Quick Reference Guide™

Microsoft Excel
for Windows® 95

Version 7.0

Karl Schwartz & Joanne Schwartz

275 Madison Avenue New York, NY 10016

Copyright 1995 by DDC Publishing, Inc.

Published by DDC Publishing, Inc.

All rights reserved, including the right to
reproduce this book or portions thereof in any
form whatsoever.
For information, address
DDC Publishing, Inc.
275 Madison Ave.
New York, New York 10016.

First DDC Publishing

10   9   8   7   6   5   4   3   2   1
Printed in the United States of America

Catalog No. XL7

ISBN: 1-56243-249-4

*Microsoft, MS, Windows, the Excel logo, the Windows logo, MS-DOS,
Access, Fox Pro, and Visual Basic are either registered trademarks or
trademarks of Microsoft Corporation.*

Screen shots reprinted with permission of Microsoft Corporation.

*Portions of the Microsoft Excel Solver program code are copyright 1990,
1991, 1992 by Frontline Systems, Inc.   Portions are copyright 1989 by
Optimal Methods, Inc.*

*IBM is a registered trademark of International Business Machines
Corporation.*

*1-2-3 and Lotus are registered trademarks of Lotus Development
Corporation. cc:Mail is a trademark of cc:Mail Inc., a wholly owned
subsidiary of Lotus Development Corporation.*

*All registered trademarks, trademarks and service marks mentioned in this
guide are the property of their respective companies.*

INTRODUCTION

Our DDC Quick Reference Guide for Microsoft® Excel
for Windows® 95 — Version 7.0 is designed to help you
perform Excel spreadsheet operations without searching
through a lengthy manual for instructions.

In this guide you will find:

- Step-by-step instructions showing you how to perform
  Excel actions easily using a mouse — we explain
  basic mouse operations on page iii.

- Procedures that include the graphic controls and symbols
  appearing on your Excel screen.

- Topics grouped together so related information is easy to
  find. (*See Table of Contents, page iv.*)

Before you begin, read page ii for advice on how best to use
this book.

We are confident our guide will help you to utilize and enjoy
Microsoft Excel for Windows 95.

Karl Schwartz and Joanne Schwartz

English Editor . . . . Ayanna Gaines
Managing Editor . . . . Kathy Berkemeyer
Design and Layout . . . . . Karl Schwartz and Joanne Schwartz

Before You Begin

If You Have Never Used a Mouse:

Read Basic Mouse Operations, page iii, for information on how to click, double-click, and drag items with a mouse.

If You Are New to Windows:

Read and practice the skills in the Getting Started section, page 1. It includes instructions for selecting menus and dialog box options, and shows you how to work with Windows elements.

If You Are New to Excel:

Read The Excel Window, page 3, to get acquainted with the basic parts of the Excel application window. Then read and practice the skills described in these important topics:

- Select Cells, page 48
- Select Sheets, page 42
- About Cells, page 244
- About Formulas, page 244
- Relative, Absolute, and Mixed Cell References, pages 244 and 245

Reference Guide Conventions

This book uses the following format conventions:

Text format	Indicates
Bold and Large	Menu names and items on a menu: • Click .... **File, Open...**
Bold	A specific name as it appears in Excel: • Select .... ☐ **Case Sensitive**
Bold and Italic	An object, object name or a major action that does not specifically appear: • Select .... ***cell(s) to delete***

Basic Mouse Operations

By default, the left mouse button is the primary mouse button. You can change the primary button and other mouse controls from Windows Control Panel. (Refer to your Windows documentation for help on how to customize a mouse.)

To point to an item:

- Move . . . . *the mouse*
  until the pointer touches desired item.
  The pointer is a graphic that moves as you move the mouse. The shape of the pointer changes, depending upon the object it is pointing to and the kinds of actions it can do.

To click an item:

1 Point . . . . *to item*

2 Quickly press and release . . . . *left mouse button*

To right-click an item:

1 Point . . . . *to item*

2 Quickly press and release . . . . *right mouse button*

To double-click an item:

1 Point . . . . *to item*

2 Press and release . . . . *left mouse button*
  twice in rapid succession.

To drag an item (drag and drop):

1 Point . . . . *to item*

2 Press *and hold* . . . . *left mouse button*
  while moving . . . . *mouse*
  The item moves as you move the mouse.

3 Release . . . . *mouse button*
  to drop item at the current location.

iv

Table of Contents

Getting Started

Toolbars

Continued ...

Table of Contents — Toolbars (continued)

Manage Workbooks

Continued ...

vi

Table of Contents (continued)

Continued ...

Table of Contents — Edit Cells (continued)

Formulas and Functions

Name Cells and Formulas

Calculate

Continued ...

viii

Table of Contents — Calculate (continued)

Pivot Tables

Continued ...

Table of Contents — Pivot Tables (continued)

Sort Data

Lists

Outlines

Continued ...

X

Table of Contents — Outlines (continued)

Format Data and Worksheets

Continued ...

Table of Contents (continued)

Continued ...

xii

Continued ...

Table of Contents (continued)

Charts

Continued ...

xiv

Continued ...

Table of Contents (continued)

Run Excel

Using Start — Programs Menu

1 Click . . . . `Start`

2 Point to . . . . `Programs ▶`

3 Point to . . . . *submenu name ▶*
containing Excel shortcut (such as Microsoft Office).

4 Click . . . . `Microsoft Excel`

Using Start — Run Command

1 Click . . . . `Start`

2 Click . . . . `Run...`

3 Type EXCEL In . . . . `Open:` `[          ▼]`

4 Click . . . . `OK`

Using a Shortcut to Excel
— FROM FOLDER CONTAINING SHORTCUT TO EXCEL —

● Double-click . . . .

`Microsoft Excel`

Using an Excel Document
— FROM FOLDER CONTAINING AN EXCEL DOCUMENT —

● Double-click . . . . `yourdoc.xls`
where yourdoc.XLS is the name of the
Excel document you want to open.

2

Set Excel Run Options

– FROM FOLDER CONTAINING SHORTCUT TO EXCEL –

1 Right-click . . . .

A shortcut menu appears.

Microsoft Excel

2 Click . . . . **P_roperties**

FROM SHORTCUT

To change how Excel starts:

- Type or edit command to start Excel in . . **Target:** ☐
  using the following examples as a model:

  EXCEL filename   *(run Excel and open specified file).*
  EXCEL /R filename *(run Excel and open specified file as read only).*
  EXCEL /E   *(run Excel and suppress creation of*
                 BOOK1.XLS).

To assign a shortcut key that lets you run or switch to Excel quickly:

- Press keys (e.g. Ctrl+E) in . . . . . . **Shortcut k_ey:** ☐
  NOTE: *Shortcut key must combine **Ctrl** and/or **Alt** and another key, such as **Ctrl + Alt + E.***

To set initial window state for Excel:

- Select desired option in . . . . **R_un:** ☐ ▼
  Options include: *Normal window, Minimized, Maximized*

3 Click . . . .   OK

The Excel Window

Use the illustration below and the terms that follow to learn about
the basic parts of the Excel application window.

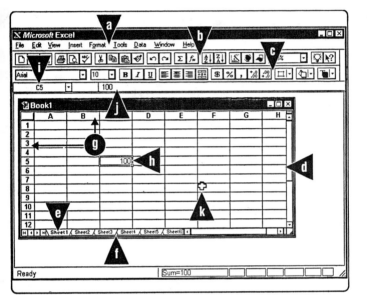

- The *Microsoft Excel application window* contains a **menu bar**[a]
  immediately below its title bar. You will use the menu bar to
  select commands the menu contains.

- Below the menu bar, Excel provides buttons on two rows
  of **toolbars**[b,c] that you can use to select commands quickly,
  without opening a menu or dialog box.

- When you first run Excel, it opens a document window called
  a **workbook**[d] (Book1) that displays the active worksheet
  (Sheet1). Each workbook contains multiple worksheets
  (Sheet1, Sheet2 . . .) in which you will enter your data and
  formulas.

Continued ...

The Excel Window (continued)

- **Sheet tabs ^f**, at the bottom of the workbook window, provide an easy way for you to switch between worksheets. The **active worksheet tab ^e** is shown in bold (Sheet1).

- **Row and column headings ^g** in a worksheet form a grid of cells. You can use these headings to select an entire row or column of cells or to change the row or column size.

- Excel names each **cell ^h** by the intersection of its row and column (cell reference). The **active cell ^h** contains a dark outline. When a cell is active, you can type data in it or edit the data the cell contains.

- Below the toolbars, Excel provides a **name box ⁱ** — drop-down list showing the name, or cell reference, of the active cell. You can also use this list to go to a specific cell quickly.

- The **formula bar ^j** provides useful tools for typing or editing cell data.

- The **mouse pointer ^k** moves as you move the mouse. Its shape will change depending upon the object it is pointing to and the kinds of actions it can do. You can use the mouse pointer to select items such as cells, menu items, toolbar buttons, and worksheets.

Quit Excel

- Click .... **File, Exit**

OR

- Press .... **Alt** + **F4**

    NOTE: If you have not saved changes made to a workbook, a message box will appear prompting you to save them.

Select Item from a Menu Bar

The menus and menu items you see in the Excel application window will depend upon the situation or the current selection. For example, if no workbook is open, Excel will display only the File and Help menus. If an embedded chart or chart worksheet is selected, Excel will show menu items for charts.

If the menu or menu item you want is not available, you may have to do one of the following:

- *Select worksheet or item appropriate to the action you want to take.*
- *Deselect object or cell.*
- *Click a cell to disable cell editing.*

1 Click . . . . *desired menu name*
Excel displays a menu.

2 Point to or click . . . . *desired menu item*

> **NOTE:** *Menu items may contain the following indicators:*
>
> ▶ *A triangle indicates a submenu will open.*
>
> ... *An ellipsis indicates another window or dialog box will open.*
>
> *key* *A key name (such as Ctrl+X) shows a fast way to perform the action without opening the menu.*
>
> ✓ *A check mark indicates the item is selected.*

To close a menu without selecting an item:

- Click . . . . *anywhere outside menu*

Menu Bar steps will be shown as:

- Click . . . . *menu name, menu item*

Select Item from a Shortcut Menu

Excel provides shortcut menus that pop up when you right-click certain items. The shortcut menu options pertain to the item.

1 Right-click . . . . ***desired item***
Excel displays a shortcut menu.

2 Click . . . . ***desired menu item***

> *NOTE: Menu items may contain the following indicators:*
>
> ▶ *A triangle indicates a submenu will open.*
>
> ... *An ellipsis indicates another window or dialog box will open.*

To close a shortcut menu without selecting an item:

• Click . . . . ***anywhere outside menu***

Shortcut Menu steps will be shown as:

---

1 Right-click . . . . ***item***
2 Click . . . . ***menu item***

Dialog Box Elements

When Excel needs additional information to complete a command, a dialog box appears. Dialog boxes may contain the following elements:

- **Command buttons** carry out actions described in the button's name such as OK .

- A **check box** ☐ provides for the selection or deselection of an option. A selected check box ☑ contains a check mark. More than one check box may be selected at a time in a group of check boxes.

- A **drop-down list box** [⠀⠀⠀⠀▾] provides a **drop-down list arrow** you can click to open and select an item in the list. Excel displays the currently selected item in the box.

- An **increment box** [⠀⠀⠀⬍] (or spin box) provides a space for typing a value. Up and down arrows (usually to the right of the box) give you a way to select a value with the mouse.

- A **list box** displays a list of items from which selections can be made. A list box may have a scroll bar that can be used to show hidden items in the list.

- An **option button** ◯ provides for the selection of one option in a group of option buttons. A selected option button ⊙ contains a dark circle.

- A **scroll bar** is a horizontal or vertical bar providing scroll arrows and a scroll box that can be used to show hidden items in a list. (Also see Scroll in a Worksheet, page 12.)

- A **text box** [⠀⠀⠀⠀] provides a space for typing in information.

- A **named tab**, such as [⠀Margins⠀], provides a way to show options related to the tab's name in the same dialog box.

Select Options in a Dialog Box

Select Item in Drop-Down List

1 Click . . . . *drop-down list arrow* ▾

If item is not in view,

- Click . . . . ▲▾

2 Click . . . . *item*
Selected item appears in the closed list.

Drop-Down List steps will be shown as:

- Select item in . . . . *list name:* ▾

Select Items in List Box

One Item

- Click . . . . *item*

If item is not in view,

a Click . . . . ▲▾

b Click . . . . *item*
Selected item is highlighted.

Consecutive Items

1 Click . . . . *first item*

2 Press <u>Shift</u> and click . . . . *last item in group*
Selected items are highlighted.

Multiple Items

- Press <u>Ctrl</u> and click . . . . *each item*
Selected items are highlighted.

List Box steps will be shown as:

- Select item(s) in . . . . *list name:* list

Select Options in a Dialog Box (continued)

Add Data to Text Box

Add New Data

1 Click in . . . . *text box name:* ☐

2 Type the data . . . . *data*
NOTE: *You can double-click existing data to select it,*
then type new data to overwrite the selection.

Add Cell Reference by Selecting it in Worksheet

1 Click in . . . . *text box name:* ☐

2 Select . . . . *cell(s)*
to reference in desired worksheet.
Excel inserts reference for selection in text box.
NOTES: *You can press* **Ctrl** *to select non-adjacent references*
in a worksheet. When you do this, Excel inserts a comma
between each reference in the text box. To select cells in another
workbook, first click anywhere on the workbook, then click the desired
sheet tab before selecting cells to add to the text box.

Text Box steps will be shown as:

• Type information in . . . . *text box name:* ☐

   OR

   Select (in worksheet)
   or type reference in . . . . *text box name:* ☐

Select or Deselect Check Box

• Click . . . . ☐ *option name*
to select it.
NOTE: *More than one check box may be selected in a group.*

OR

• Click . . . . ☑ *option name*
to deselect it.

Check Box steps will be shown as:

• Select or deselect . . . . ☐ *option name*

Select Options in a Dialog Box (continued)

Select Option Button

- Click . . . . ◯ *option name*
  to select it.
  NOTE: Only one option button may be selected in a group.

Option Button steps will be shown as:

- Select . . . . ◯ *option name*

Select Command Button

- Click . . . . [command name]
  Clicked command button carries out the command action.

Command Button steps will be shown as:

- Click . . . . [command name]

Type or Select Value in Increment (Spin) Box

1 Click in . . . . [⬦]

2 Type desired value . . . . *number*
  The typed or selected value appears in the box.

OR

- Click . . . . *up or down increment arrows* [⬦]
  until desired value appears.
  The typed or selected value appears in the box.

Increment Box steps will be shown as:

- Type or select value in . . *increment box name:* [⬦]

Select Options in a Dialog Box (continued)

Select a Tab
Some dialog boxes include tabs that group related options.

- Click .... | tab name |

   Selected tabs show related options in dialog box.

Select Tab will be shown as:

FROM TAB NAME

Get Help in a Dialog Box

1 Click .... ***Help button*** [?]

2 Click .... ***dialog box option***

   Windows displays help for the item.

Undo a Command

NOTE: *To successfully undo a command, undo before another command is selected. Not all commands can be undone.*

- Click .... ***Undo button*** [↶]

   on Standard toolbar.

OR

- Click .... **Edit, Undo . . .**

Repeat a Command

NOTE: *To successfully repeat a command, repeat before another command is selected. Not all commands can be repeated.*

- Click .... ***Repeat button*** [↷]

   on Standard toolbar.

OR

- Click .... **Edit, Repeat . . .**

Scroll in a Worksheet

Scrolling moves an area of data into view. The size of the scroll boxes are proportional to the dimensions of the used worksheet. Excel shows the destination row or column (ScrollTips) when you drag a scroll box.

scroll bar

scroll box   scroll arrow

Left or Right One Column

• Click . . . . *left or right scroll arrow*

Up or Down One Row

• Click . . . . *up or down scroll arrow*

First Column

• Drag . . . . *horizontal scroll box*
  to the extreme left of scroll bar.

Any Column Containing Data

• Drag . . . . *horizontal scroll box*
  left or right.

First Row

• Drag . . . . *vertical scroll box*
  to the top of scroll bar.

Any Row Containing Data

• Drag . . . . *vertical scroll box*
  up or down.

One Screen Up or Down

• Click . . . . *vertical scroll bar*
  above or below scroll box.

One Screen Right or Left

• Click . . . . *horizontal scroll bar*
  to right or left of scroll box.

Get Help

1   Click . . . . **Help, Microsoft Excel Help Topics**

FROM CONTENTS

a   Double-click desired . . . . 📖 *topic category name*

    NOTE: *Repeat this step until desired topic appears.*

b   Double-click desired . . . . ? *topic name*

FROM INDEX

a   Type the first few letters of item to look up in . . .

b   Double-click desired item in . . . . *list box*

FROM FIND

a   Type or select the word(s) to find in . . . . .

b   Click matching word(s) in . . . . *middle list box*

c   Double-click desired topic in . . . . *bottom list box*

FROM ANSWER WIZARD

a   Type your question in . . . .

b   Click . . . .   Search

c   Double-click desired topic in . . . . *bottom list box*

2   Read or follow prompts provided.

3   Click . . . .   Help Topics

    to return to Help Topics.

    OR

    Click . . . . *close button* ☒

    to close the Help windows.

Window Controls

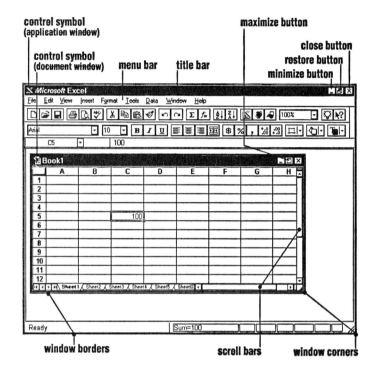

control symbol
(application window)

control symbol
(document window)　　menu bar　　title bar

maximize button

close button
restore button
minimize button

window borders　　　　scroll bars　　window corners

- The **control symbol** provides access to a menu containing commands to help you control the window.

- The Excel **application window** contains **document windows** called workbooks. The Excel application window has the Microsoft Excel icon as its control symbol and also contains a menu bar. A workbook window, such as Book1 in the illustration, has the Excel document icon as its control symbol.

- The **menu bar** displays menu names and appears immediately below the title bar in an application window.

- The **title bar** displays the window name. You can drag a window's title bar to move the window, or you can double-click it to maximize/restore the window's size.

Continued ...

Window Controls (continued)

- **Scroll bars** are controls you can use to display areas in a window that are presently not in view.

- The **close button** ☒ is a box you can click to close the window.

- The **maximize button** 🗖 is a box you can click to increase the window to its largest size.

- The **restore button** 🗗 is a box appearing in a maximized window. You can click it to restore the window to its previous size.

- The **minimize button** 🗕 is a box you can click to reduce the window to a button on the taskbar (for application windows) or a button in the application's workspace (for document windows).

- A **window border or corner** marks the edges of the window. You can drag a window's border or corner to change the size of the window. An easy way to size a window is to drag the sizing corner located in the bottom-right corner of a window.

Restore a Maximized Window

Restores a maximized window to its previous size. After restoring a window, the maximize button appears.

Using Restore Button

- Click desired window's . . . . *restore button* 🗗

Using Title Bar

- Double-click window's . . . . ▐ *Title bar* ▌

Excel Window Using Taskbar

1 Right-click . . . . *Microsoft Excel button* on taskbar.

2 Click . . . . **R̲estore**

Change Size of a Window

NOTE: *A maximized window must be restored (page 15) before you can size it.*

By Dragging

1 Point to . . . . ***border or corner of window***
to size.
Pointer becomes one of the following: ↔↘

2 Drag . . . . ***window outline***
to desired size.

3 Repeat steps above until desired size is obtained.

Using Keyboard

NOTE: *This method is useful when the border of the window you want to size is not accessible.*

1 Press . . . . **Alt**+**Space**
to open Excel's control menu.

   OR

   Press . . . . **Alt**+**−**
   to open selected workbook's control menu.

2 Select Size . . . . **S**

3 Press . . . . **↕**
once, in direction of border to change.

4 Press . . . . **↕**
until the window's border is the desired size.

5 Press . . . . **↵**
to end sizing.

Move a Window

NOTE: A maximized window must be restored (page 15) before you can move it.

By Dragging

*   Drag window's . . . . | *Title bar* |
    to new location.

Using Keyboard

NOTE: This method is useful when the title bar of the window you want to move is off the screen.

1 Press . . . . |Alt|+|Space|
to open Excel's control menu.

   OR

   Press . . . . |Alt|+|—|
   to open selected workbook's control menu.

2 Select <u>M</u>ove . . . . |M|

3 Press . . . . |↕|
until the window is positioned as desired.

4 Press . . . . |↵|
to end moving.

Move a Minimized Workbook

*   Drag . . . . *workbook button*
    in Excel's workspace to new location.

18

Minimize a Window

Reduces the Excel application window to a button on the taskbar, or workbook windows to buttons in Excel's workspace.

Using Minimize Button

- Click desired window's . . . . **minimize button** ⬜

Using Keyboard

NOTE: This method is useful when the title bar of the window you want to minimize is off the screen.

1 Press . . . . **Alt** + **Space**
to open Excel's control menu.

OR

Press . . . . **Alt** + ⬛
to open selected workbook's control menu.

2 Select Mi<u>n</u>imize . . . . **N**

Excel Window Using Taskbar

1 Right-click . . . . **Microsoft Excel button**
on taskbar.

2 Click . . . . **Mi<u>n</u>imize**

Maximize a Window

Expands Excel window to fill the desktop, and workbook windows to fill Excel's workspace. After maximizing a window, the restore button appears.

Using Maximize Button

• Click desired window's . . . . *maximize button* ⬜

Using Keyboard

NOTE: This method is useful when the title bar of the window you want to maximize is off the screen.

1 Press . . . . **Alt** + **Space**
to open Excel's control menu.

OR

Press . . . . **Alt** + **▬**
to open selected workbook's control menu.

2 Select Ma<u>x</u>imize . . . . **X**

Using Title Bar

• Double-click window's . . . . **Title bar**

The Excel Window Using Taskbar

When you minimize the Excel window, it appears as a button on the taskbar. You can open and maximize Excel quickly using this procedure.

1 Right-click . . . . *Microsoft Excel button*
on taskbar.

2 Click . . . . **Ma<u>x</u>imize**

Close a Window

Using Close Button

- Click desired window's . . . . *close button* ☒

Using Keyboard

- Press . . . . **Alt** + **F4**
  to close Excel and all open workbooks.

OR

- Press . . . . **Ctrl** + **W**
  to close selected workbook.

The Excel Window Using Taskbar
When you minimize the Excel window, it appears as a button on the taskbar.
You can close Excel quickly using this procedure.

1 Right-click . . . . *Microsoft Excel button*
  on taskbar.

2 Click . . . . **C**lose

Open a Minimized Window

Workbook Window

1 Click desired . . . . *workbook button*
  in Excel's workspace.

2 Click . . . . **R**estore
  OR
  Click . . . . **Ma**x**imize**

Excel Window

1 Right-click . . . . *Microsoft Excel button*
  on taskbar.

2 Click . . . . **R**estore
  OR
  Click . . . . **Ma**x**imize**

Show Name and Purpose
of Any Toolbar Button

- Point to and rest pointer on .... ***desired button on toolbar***
  *Excel displays button name on the toolbar and information about the tool
  on the left side of the status bar.*

Open Toolbar Shortcut Menu

1 Right-click . . . . ***blank area on toolbar***

2 Select . . . . ***desired menu option:***
  *Built-in toolbars (Standard, Formatting, Chart, Drawing,
  Forms, Visual Basic, Auditing, WorkGroup), Toolbars..., Customize...*

Show or Hide a Toolbar

1 Click . . . . **View, Toolbars...**
  (Also see Open Toolbar Shortcut Menu, above.)

2 Select or deselect desired toolbar(s) in . . . . **Toolbars:** *list*
  Toolbars include: *Standard, Formatting, Query and Pivot,
  Chart, Drawing, TipWizard, Forms, Stop Recording, Visual Basic,
  Auditing, WorkGroup, Microsoft, Full Screen*

3 Click . . . . | OK |

Move a Toolbar

*You can dock a toolbar (between the menu bar and the formula bar or on the
edges of the Excel window), or have it float as a separate window. Toolbars
containing a drop-down list (i.e., the Formatting toolbar) cannot be docked on
the left or right edge of the Excel window.*

1 Point to . . . . ***blank area on toolbar***
  OR
  Point to . . . . ***title bar of floating toolbar***

2 Drag . . . . ***toolbar outline***
  to desired position.

Switch Between Floating or Docking a Toolbar

• Double-click . . . . ***blank area on toolbar***

Size a Floating Toolbar

*(See **Change Size of a Window**, page 16.)*

Set General Toolbar Options

1 Click . . . . **View, Toolbars...**
  *(Also see **Open Toolbar Shortcut Menu**, page 21.)*

2 Select or deselect . . . . ***Toolbar options:***
  Color Toolbars, Large Buttons, Show ToolTips

3 Click . . . . `   OK   `

Create a Customized Toolbar

1 Click . . . . **View, Toolbars...**
  *(Also see **Open Toolbar Shortcut Menu**, page 21.)*

2 Type a unique toolbar name in . . . . **Toolbar Name:** `         `

3 Click . . . . `  New  `
  Excel displays an empty toolbar and opens the Customize dialog box.

To add a button to the new toolbar:

  a Select a category in . . . . **Categories:** *list*

   To see a button's description:

   1. Click desired button in . . . . **Buttons** *box*

   2. Read description at bottom of dialog box.

  b Drag . . . . ***desired button***
   onto . . . . ***new toolbar***

  c Repeat steps **a** and **b**, as needed.

4 Click . . . . `  Close  `

Delete a Customized Toolbar

1 Click . . . . **View, Toolbars...**
(Also see Open Toolbar Shortcut Menu, page 21.)

2 Select toolbar to delete in . . . . **Toolbars:** *list*

3 Click . . . . | Delete |

4 Click . . . . | OK |
to confirm deletion.

5 Click . . . . | OK |

Restore a Built-in Toolbar

1 Click . . . . **View, Toolbars...**
(Also see Open Toolbar Shortcut Menu, page 21.)

2 Select name of built-in toolbar to restore in . . . **Toolbars:** *list*

3 Click . . . . | Reset |
NOTE: *If you do not see the Reset button, you have selected a customized toolbar. Customized toolbars cannot be reset.*

4 Click . . . . | OK |

Change Width of a Toolbar's Drop-Down List

1 Right-click . . . . *blank area on toolbar*

2 Click . . . . **Customize...**

3 Click . . . . *border of* | ▾ |
on toolbar to change.
Excel highlights drop-down list border.

4 Point to . . . . *left or right border*
of drop-down list to size.
Pointer becomes a ↔ when positioned correctly.

5 Drag . . . . *box outline left or right*

6 Click . . . . | Close |

Move a Toolbar Button

*Groups a button with other buttons, adds space between buttons, moves a
button to a new position on a toolbar, and moves a button to another toolbar.
If you are moving a button to another toolbar, both toolbars must be in view.*

1   Right-click . . . . *blank area on toolbar*

2   Click . . . . **Customize...**

3   Drag . . . . *button on toolbar*
        to desired location on current or other toolbar.

4   Click . . . . [Close]

Copy a Toolbar Button

*NOTE: When copying a button to another toolbar, be sure to have both
toolbars in view.*

1   Right-click . . . . *blank area on toolbar*

2   Click . . . . **Customize...**

3   Press Ctrl and drag . . . . *button on toolbar*
        to desired location on destination toolbar.

4   Click . . . . [Close]

Use TipWizard

Turn TipWizard On or Off

•   Click . . . . *TipWizard button*
    *When on, Excel displays tips in the TipWizard box above the formula
    bar for easier ways to do your work.*

View Other Tips for the Current Work Session

•   Click . . . . *up and down arrows*
    to the right of the TipWizard box.

Add or Remove Toolbar Buttons

1 Right-click . . . . *blank area on toolbar*

2 Click . . . . **Customize...**

To add a button:

a Select a category in . . . . <u>C</u>ategories: *list*

To see a button's description:

1. Click desired button in . . . . **Buttons** *box*

2. Read description at bottom of dialog box.

b Drag . . . . *desired button*
to desired position on destination toolbar.

c Repeat steps **a** and **b**, as needed.

To remove a button:

• Drag . . . . *button off toolbar*

3 Click . . . . | Close |

Copy Image of a Toolbar Button to Another Button

NOTE: Both the source and destination buttons must be in view.

1 Right-click . . . . *blank area on toolbar*

2 Click . . . . **Customize...**

3 Click . . . . *source button on toolbar*

4 Click . . . . <u>E</u>dit, <u>C</u>opy Button Image

5 Click . . . . *destination button on toolbar*

6 Click . . . . <u>E</u>dit, <u>P</u>aste Button Image

7 Click . . . . | Close |

Edit Image of a Toolbar Button

1 Right-click . . . . *blank area on toolbar*

2 Click . . . . **Customize...**

3 Right-click . . . . *button on toolbar to change*

4 Click . . . . **Edit Button Image...**

To erase entire image:

● Click . . . . | Clear |

To change or add colors:

a Select a color in . . . . **Colors** *box*

b Click or drag through . . . . *each pixel to color* in Picture box.

c Repeat steps **a** and **b**, as desired.

To move image:

● Click . . . . *arrow button* in direction to move image.

5 Click . . . . | OK |

6 Click . . . . | Close |

Restore Image of a Toolbar Button

1 Right-click . . . . *blank area on toolbar*

2 Click . . . . **Customize...**

3 Right-click . . . . *button on toolbar to restore*

4 Click . . . . **Reset Button Image**

5 Click . . . . | Close |

Open New Workbook

Open New Workbook Based on Default Template

- Click . . . . *New Workbook button* 🗋
  on Standard toolbar.

Open New Workbook Based on Saved or Built-in Template

1 Click . . . . **File, New**
2 Click . . . . *tab containing the template*
   NOTE: *The* **General** *tab contains the default Workbook and templates you have saved to the \EXCEL\XLSTART folder. The* **Spreadsheet Solutions** *tab contains built-in templates. Other tabs will appear if you have saved templates in folders created in the \TEMPLATES folder.*

3 Select desired template in . . . . *list*
4 Click . . . . `OK`

Open Recently Opened Workbook

By default, Excel lists the last four workbooks you worked with near the bottom of the File menu.

- Click . . . . **File,** *desired workbook name*

Open Duplicate Workbook Window

1 Select . . . . *workbook window to duplicate*
2 Click . . . . **Window, New Window**

Select a Workbook

- Click . . . . *workbook window*

OR

- Click . . . . **Window,** *name of workbook*
  NOTE: *Excel displays the names of recently opened workbooks near the bottom of the Window menu.*

Open Workbooks

1 Click .... ***Open button*** 🖼

on Standard toolbar.

OR

Click .... **File, Open...**

To list specific file formats to open or import:

- Select file type in .... **Files of type:** [＿＿＿＿＿ ▼]

  File types may include: All Files, Microsoft Excel Files, Text Files,
  Lotus 1-2-3 Files, QuattroPro/DOS Files, Microsoft Works Files,
  dBase Files, Microsoft Excel 4.0 Macros, Microsoft Excel 4.0 Charts,
  Microsoft Excel Workbooks, Worksheets, Workspaces, Templates,
  Add-ins, Toolbars, SYLK Files, Data Interchange Format, Backup Files

2 Display contents of folder containing document(s)
to open (page 29).

3 Select .... ***document(s) to open***

  NOTES: You can select multiple documents by holding
  Ctrl *while clicking each document you want to open*
  in the documents list.

  If you open a template, Excel opens a copy of the template
  and adds a number to the end of its workbook name.

To open document as read-only:

- Select .... ☐ **Read Only**

4 Click .... [Open]

Open Original Template File

1 Click .... ***Open button*** 🖼

on Standard toolbar.

2 Select Templates (*xlt) in ..... **Files of type:** [＿＿＿＿＿ ▼]

3 Select .... ***template file to open***

  NOTE: Use the Open dialog box to display contents of folder
  containing desired template file (page 29).

4 Press Shift and click .... [Open]

Use the Open Dialog Box

You can use the Open dialog box to filter, preview, locate, print, and manage Excel documents displayed in the documents list.
IMPORTANT: Files displayed in the documents list depend on criteria settings at the bottom of the dialog box. See List Only Documents Meeting Your Criteria, page 31, and List All Excel Documents (Clear Criteria), page 31.

Display Contents of any Folder

1 Select drive containing folder in . . . **Look in:** [⬚ ▾]

    NOTE: You can also select the desktop, a folder on the desktop, or Network Neighborhood to open folders contained in those locations.

2 Double-click . . . . ▢ *folder name*
in documents list containing items to display.

Display Contents of Folder(s) by Typing a Path

• Type path to folder in . . . . **File name:** [⬚ ▾]

    NOTE: A path is a notation that indicates the location of documents. You can type multiple paths if you separate them with a semicolon (;).
    EXAMPLES:
    Shared folder on a network `\\computername\sharename`
    Folder on drive c `c:\foldername\subfoldername`

Display Contents of Parent Folder

• Click . . . . *Up One Level button* [t..]

Change View of Items in Documents List

• Select . . . . *desired button on toolbar:*

    • Click . . . . *List button* [▤]
    to list only document names.

    • Click . . . . *Details button* [▦]
    to list document names, size, type, and date modified.

    • Click . . . . *Properties button* [▥]
    to show properties of selected document.

    • Click . . . . *Preview button* [▥]
    to preview selected document.

Use the Open Dialog Box (continued)

Sort Items in Documents List
Using Column Headings

1 Change view of items to Details, Properties, or Preview (page 29).

2 Click . . . . **column heading**
in documents list to sort by.
NOTE: In Details view, you can sort by Name, Size, Type, Modified.

3 Repeat step 2 to reverse the sort order for the same column.

Using Commands and Settings Button

1 Click . . . . **Commands and Settings button** 🔲

2 Click . . . . **Sorting...**

3 Select sort option in . . . . **Sort files by:** ⌐_____▾⌐

4 Select . . . . ◯ **Ascending**
OR
Select . . . . ◯ **Descending**

5 Click . . . . ▢ OK ▢

Add Items to Favorites Folder
Adds shortcuts to the selected folder, selected document, or the current folder (in Look in box) to the Favorites folder. You can then go to these items quickly using the Look in Favorites button.

1 If adding an item (folder or document), select it.

2 Click . . . . **Add to Favorites button** 🔳

3 Select . . . . **Add 'current folder name' to Favorites**
OR
Select . . . . **Add Selected Item to Favorites**

Look in Favorites Folder

1 Click . . . . **Look in Favorites button** 🔳
Shortcuts to folders and documents appear in documents list.

2 Double-click . . . . 🗂 **folder shortcut**
to view items in the folder.
NOTE: If you double-click a shortcut to a document, Excel opens it.

Use the Open Dialog Box (continued)

List Only Documents Meeting Your Criteria

Lists documents (in current folder) that meet your criteria. The name of the current folder appears in the Look in box.

1 Set criteria:

Filename

- Type part of filename, entire
  filename or filespec in . . . . . **File name:** [_____|▼]

  NOTE: *A filespec is file name pattern in which wildcard characters (* ?) can be used to represent any character (?) or group of characters (*).*

  EXAMPLES: `Chapt??.doc` `Chapt7.*`

File type

- Select desired file type in . . **Files of type:** [_____|▼]

Text or file property

- Type or select text in . . **Text or property:** [_____|▼]

  NOTE: *Enclose text in quotation marks (" ").*

Date

- Select time in . . . . **Last modified:** [_____|▼]

2 Click . . . . [Find Now]

  NOTE: *You can stop the search for files meeting your criteria by clicking the Stop button.*

List All Excel Documents (Clear Criteria)

- Click . . . . [New Search]

Print Documents in Documents List

1 Select . . . . *document(s) to print*

  NOTES: *You can select multiple documents by holding **Ctrl** while clicking each document you want to print in the documents list.*

2 Click . . . . *Commands and Settings button* 🗗

3 Click . . . . **Print**

Use the Open Dialog Box (continued)

View or Edit Document Properties

1 Select .... *desired document*

2 Click .... *Commands and Settings button* 🗒

3 Click .... **Properties**

4 View or make changes as desired.

5 Click .... | OK |

Show or Hide Subfolders in Documents List

By default, Excel shows only Excel documents in the current folder.
If you select the option that follows, Excel shows the contents of all
folders (below the current folder) that contain Excel documents.
The documents are grouped by folder. To display the list of documents
in multiple folders as a single list, see Ungroup Documents by Folder
in Documents List, *below.*

1 Click .... *Commands and Settings button* 🗒

2 Click .... **Search Subfolders**
   to select or deselect.

Ungroup Documents by Folder in Documents List

Displays documents in more than one folder in a single list.

1 Show subfolders in documents list (see above).

2 Click .... *Commands and Settings button* 🗒

3 Click .... **Group files by folder**
   to deselect the option.

Search for Documents using Saved Search

NOTE: See Use Advanced Search to Find a Document, *on next page,*
for information about saving search criteria.

1 Click .... *Commands and Settings button* 🗒

2 Click .... **Saved Searches** ▸

3 Click .... *desired search name*

Use the Open Dialog Box (continued)

Use Advanced Search to Find a Document

Add search criteria

1 Select . . . . ○ A**n**d or ○ O**r**

2 Select property in . . . . **Property:** [▼]

3 Select condition for property in . . . **Condition:** [▼]

4 Type value in . . . . **Val**u**e:** [   ]

5 Click . . . . [**A**dd to List]

6 Repeat steps 1–5 for each criterion to add.

7 Select or deselect . . . . ☐ **Match a**l**l word forms**

    OR

    Select or deselect . . . . ☐ **M**atch case

Delete search criteria

• Select criterion to delete, then click . . . . [Delete]

Return to default search criteria

• Click . . . . [Ne**w** Search]

Define search location

1 Select location to search in . . . . . . **Look** i**n:** [▼]

2 Select or deselect . . . . ☐ **Searc**h **subfolders**

Save search

1 Click . . . . [**S**ave Search...]

2 Type name for search in . . **Name for this Search:** [   ]

3 Click . . . . [OK]

Open a saved search

1 Click . . . . [O**p**en Search...]

2 Select search to open in . . . . *list*

3 Click . . . . [**O**pen]

4 Edit or use the search as desired.

Search using current criteria

• Click . . . . [**F**ind Now]

Use the Open Dialog Box (continued)

Right-Click Options for Items in Documents List

1 Right-click . . . . *desired document or folder*
A shortcut menu appears.
NOTE: *Items on menu depend upon selection in list.*

2 Click appropriate shortcut menu item.
Document options include: Copy, Create Shortcut, Cut, Delete, Open,
Open Read Only, Print, Properties, Quick View, Rename, Send To
Folder options include: Copy, Create Shortcut, Cut, Delete, Explore,
Open, Properties, Rename, Send To, Sharing

Arrange Workbook Windows

1 Click . . . . **Window, Arrange...**

2 Select . . . . *Arrange option:*
Tiled, Horizontal, Vertical, Cascade

To arrange the active workbook's windows only:

• Select . . . . □ **Windows of Active Workbook**

3 Click . . . . | OK |

Arrange Minimized Workbooks

1 Click . . . . *any workbook button*
NOTE: Ignore display of the button's control menu.

2 Click . . . . **Window, Arrange Icons**
Excel arranges workbook buttons on the bottom of the workspace.

Hide a Workbook

Hides a workbook from view, but does not close it.

1 Select . . . . *workbook to hide*

2 Click . . . . **Window, Hide**

Unhide a Workbook

1 Click . . . . **W**indow, **U**nhide...

   NOTE: If the Window menu is not available,
   open a new workbook to access the menu.

2 Select workbook to unhide in . . . . . . **U**nhide Workbook: *list*

3 Click . . . . `OK`

Close Active Workbook Window

• Click . . . . **F**ile, **C**lose

OR

• Click . . . . *workbook's close button* `X`

NOTE: If you have not saved changes made to the workbook,
Excel will prompt you to save them.

Close All Open Workbooks

1 Press **Shift** and click . . . .**F**ile

2 Click . . . . **C**lose All

   NOTE: If you have not saved changes made to the workbooks,
   Excel will prompt you to save them.

Save Workspace

Saves the names and the current arrangement of all open workbooks in a
workspace (.XLW) file. When you open a workspace file, Excel uses this file
to open all the workbooks in one step.

1 Click . . . . **F**ile, Save **W**orkspace...

2 Select . . . . *folder to receive workspace file*

   NOTE: Use procedures in **Use the Save As Dialog Box** *(page 38)*
   to select folder to receive workspace file.

3 Type name of workspace file in . . . . . **File **n**ame:** [   ]

4 Click . . . . `Save`

   Excel will prompt you to save changes made to each open workbook.

Save Workbook Again

Saves the active workbook again using the same name, format, and folder location.

- Click . . . . **Save button** 🖬
  on Standard toolbar.

OR

- Click . . . . **File, Save**

If Save As dialog box appears,
NOTE: The Save As dialog box will appear if you have not previously saved the file, or if you opened the file as read-only.

a Select (page 38) . . . . *folder to receive document*

b Type workbook name in . . . . **File name:** ⬚

c Click . . . . | Save |

Set Automatic Saving of Workbooks

1 Click . . . . **Tools, AutoSave...**
   *NOTE: If AutoSave does not appear on the Tools menu,
   see Install or Remove an Add-In, page 179.*

To enable/disable AutoSave:

- Select or deselect . . . . ☐ **Automatic Save Every**

To set time interval for AutoSave:

- Type number of minutes in . . . . ⬚ **Minutes**

To automatically save active workbook only:

- Select . . . . ◯ **Save Active Workbook Only**

To automatically save all open workbooks:

- Select . . . . ◯ **Save All Open Workbooks**

To enable/disable prompt before automatic save:

- Select or deselect . . . . ☐ **Prompt Before Saving**

2 Click . . . . | OK |

Save Active Workbook As

1 Click . . . . **File, Save As...**

2 Select (page 38) . . . . *folder to receive workbook*

3 Type workbook name in . . . . **File name:** [   ]

To change file type, save as template or export:

- Select desired file type in . . **Save as type:** [▼]

  File types may include: Microsoft Excel workbooks and
  worksheets, Templates, Text Files, Lotus 1-2-3 Files,
  dBase Files, SYLK, DIF

  NOTE: If you save a template to the EXCEL\XLSTART folder,
  it will appear in the list of templates in the General tab
  when you open a new workbook using the File, New command.

To set other options:

a Click . . . . [Options...]

  To create a backup of previous version when saving:

  - Select . . . . ☐ **Always Create Backup**

  To password protect workbook:

  - Type password in . . . **Protection Password:** [   ]

  To prevent unauthorized users from saving workbook:

  - Type password
    in . . . . **Write Reservation Password:** [   ]

  To recommend document be opened as read-only:

  - Select . . . . ☐ **Read-Only Recommended**

b Click . . . . [OK]

c If prompted, reenter password(s).

4 Click . . . . [Save]

Use the Save As Dialog Box

Most of the time, you will use the Save As dialog box to select or create a folder in which to store a document. You can also use the following procedures from the Save As dialog box:

- *Change View of Items in Documents List (page 29).*
- *Right-Click Options for Items in Documents List (page 34).*
- *Sort Items in Documents List (page 30).*
- *View or Edit Document Properties (page 32).*

Select Folder to Receive Document

1 Select drive containing folder in ... **Save in:** [_____|▼]

> *NOTE: You can also select the desktop, a folder on the desktop, or Network Neighborhood to open folders contained in those locations.*

2 Double-click .... 📁 *folder name*
in documents list.

3 Repeat step 2 until folder to receive document is current (appears in **Save in** box).

Select Folder to Receive Document by Typing a Path

- Type path to folder in .... **File name:** [_____|▼]

> *EXAMPLES:*
> *Shared folder on a network* \\computername\sharename
> *Folder on drive c* c:\foldername\subfoldername

Select Parent Folder

- Click .... *Up One Level button* [t..]

Look in Favorites Folder

NOTE: See Add Items to Favorites Folder page 30.

1 Click .... *Look in Favorites button* [✳]

> *Shortcuts to folders and documents appear in documents list.*

2 Double-click .... 📁 *folder shortcut*
to select that folder.

Create Folder to Receive Document

1 Select folder in which new folder will be created.

2 Click .... *Create New Folder button* [📁*]

View or Edit Workbook Properties

1 Click . . . . **File, Properties**
to edit properties of active workbook.

OR

– FROM "OPEN" OR "SAVE AS" DIALOG BOX –

a Right-click . . . . *desired document*

b Click . . . . **Properties**

> **FROM GENERAL**

• View items.
  General items include: *Type, Location, Size, MS-DOS Name, Created, Modified, Accessed, Attributes*

> **FROM SUMMARY**

a View or edit items.
  Summary items include: *Title, Subject, Author, Manager, Company, Category, Keywords, Comments*

b Select or deselect . . . . ☐ **Save Preview Picture**
  (Not available from Open or Save As dialog box.)

> **FROM STATISTICS**

• View items.
  Statistics items include: *Created, Modified, Accessed, Printed, Last Saved By, Revision Number, Total Editing Time*

> **FROM CONTENTS**

• View components (such as worksheets and chart sheet names) the file is made of.

> **FROM CUSTOM**

• Add or delete custom properties for the file.
  Each property includes: *Name, Type, Value*

2 Click . . . . | OK |

Set General Workbook Options

Sets default workbook options, such as the standard font and number of sheets in a workbook.

1 Click . . . . **Tools, Options...**

⌐────────────── FROM GENERAL ──────────────⌐

To set reference style:

● Select . . . . **Reference Style option:**
  A1 (default), R1C1 (columns and rows are labeled with numbers)

To set menu options:

● Select or deselect . . . . **Menu options:**
  Recently Used File List, Microsoft Excel 4.0 Menus

To set Excel to ignore DDE requests:

● Select . . . . □ **Ignore Other Applications**

To set Excel to prompt for summary info when saving a new workbook:

● Select . . . . □ **Prompt for Properties**

To reset TipWizard:

● Select . . . . □ **Reset TipWizard**

To specify number of sheets in new workbook:

● Type or select
  number in . . . . **Sheets in New Workbook:** [⇕]

To set standard font:

● Select font in . . . . **Standard Font:** [▼]

To set standard font size:

● Type or select font size in . . . . **Size:** [▼]

To set default file location:

● Type path in . . . . **Default File Location:** [   ]

Continued ...

Set General Workbook Options (continued)

To specify an alternate startup location:

Sets an additional directory location (in addition to XLSTART)
where you can store files that will open automatically, or
templates that will be available in the New dialog box.

• Type path in.. **Alternate Startup File Location:** ⬚

To specify user name:

Adds the name you specify to file sharing, summary information,
scenario, and view dialogs the next time you start Excel.

• Type name in . . . . **User Name:** ⬚

2 Click . . . . ▢ OK

Manage Sheets in Workbooks

By default, new workbooks contain worksheets labeled Sheet1, Sheet2 etc.
You can delete, rename, move, copy, and hide sheets. You can also insert
sheets of the following types: Worksheet, Chart, MS Excel 4.0 Macro,
Module, and Dialog.

workbook name

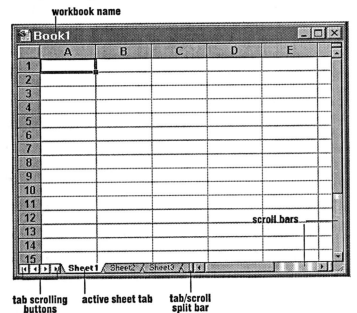

tab scrolling   **active sheet tab**   **tab/scroll**
buttons   **split bar**

42

Select Sheets

Selects the following sheet types: Worksheet, Chart, MS Excel 4.0 Macro, Module, and Dialog.

NOTE: *You select sheets by clicking their sheet tabs, located on the bottom of the workbook window. Selected sheet tabs are white; the active sheet tab is bold. Use the tab scrolling buttons (illustrated below) to view hidden sheet tabs. If no sheets are visible, see* **Set View Options**, *page 179.*

IMPORTANT: *When you group worksheets, entries and formatting applied to one worksheet are duplicated on all worksheets in the group.*

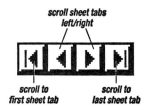

scroll sheet tabs
left/right

scroll to
first sheet tab

scroll to
last sheet tab

Select <u>One</u> Sheet

1 If necessary, click . . . . . ***tab scrolling buttons*** |◄|◄|►|►|
to scroll hidden sheet tab into view.

2 Click . . . . ＼Sheet #／
(*Sheet # is the name of the sheet to select.*)

Select (Group) <u>All</u> Sheets

1 Right-click . . . . ＼Sheet #／
(*Sheet # is the name of any sheet.*)

2 Click . . . . **Select All Sheets**

Select (Group) <u>Consecutive</u> Sheets

1 If necessary, click . . . . . ***tab scrolling buttons*** |◄|◄|►|►|
to scroll hidden sheet tabs into view.

2 Click . . . . ＼Sheet #／
(*Sheet # is the name of the first sheet to select.*)

3 Press <u>Shift</u> and click . . . . ＼Sheet #／
(*Sheet # is the name of the last sheet in group to select.*)
[Group] appears in title bar.

Continued ...

Select Sheets (continued)

Select (Group) <u>Non-Consecutive</u> Sheets

1 If necessary, click . . . . . *tab scrolling buttons* [◄◄][◄][►][►►]
to scroll hidden sheet tabs into view.

2 Click . . . . `\Sheet #/`
(*Sheet #* is the name of the first sheet to select.)

3 Press <u>Ctrl</u> and click each . . . . `\Sheet #/`
(*Sheet #* is the name of each sheet to select.)
[Group] appears in title bar.

Deselect Grouped Sheets

• Click . . . . `\Sheet #/`
(*Sheet #* is the name of any sheet that is not in group.)

OR

1 Right-click . . . . `\Sheet #/`
(*Sheet #* is the name of a sheet in group.)

2 Click . . . . **Ungroup Sheets**

Hide a Sheet

NOTE: *If a workbook has only one sheet, the sheet can not be hidden.*

1 Select . . . . *sheet to hide*

2 Click . . . . **F<u>o</u>rmat, S<u>h</u>eet ►, <u>H</u>ide**

Unhide a Sheet

1 Click . . . . **Format, Sheet ▸, Unhide..**

2 Select sheet to unhide in . . . . **Unhide Sheet:** *list*

3 Click . . . . $\boxed{\text{OK}}$

Insert Sheets

Inserts blank sheets or templates into workbook.

Insert One Sheet

1 Right-click . . . . $\diagdown\overline{\text{Sheet \#}}\diagup$
   (*Sheet #* is the name of sheet before which
   new sheet will be inserted.)

2 Click . . . . **Insert...**

   – FROM ANY TAB IN "INSERT" DIALOG BOX –

3 Double-click sheet or template to insert in . . . . *list*

   If chart was selected,

   • Follow the ChartWizard (page 193) prompts.
   Excel inserts sheet and makes the new sheet active.

Insert Multiple Sheets

1 Select . . . . **consecutive number of sheets**
   to indicate the number and location of sheets to insert.

2 Right-click . . . . $\diagdown\overline{\text{Sheet \#}}\diagup$
   (*Sheet #* is a selected sheet before which
   new sheets will be inserted.)

3 Click . . . . **Insert...**

   – FROM ANY TAB IN "INSERT" DIALOG BOX –

4 Double-click sheet or template to insert in . . . . *list*

   If chart was selected,

   • Follow the ChartWizard (page 193) prompts.
   Excel inserts sheet and makes the new sheet active.

Delete Sheets

Delete One Sheet

1 Right-click . . . . `\Sheet #/`
(*Sheet #* is the name of sheet to delete.)

2 Click . . . . **Delete**

3 Click . . . . `OK`

Delete Multiple Sheets

1 Select . . . . *sheets to delete*

2 Right-click . . . . `\Sheet #/`
(*Sheet #* is the name of a selected sheet.)

3 Click . . . . **Delete**

4 Click . . . . `OK`

Rename a Sheet

1 Double-click . . . . `\Sheet #/`
(*Sheet #* is the name of sheet to rename.)

OR

  a Right-click . . . . `\Sheet #/`
    (*Sheet #* is the name of sheet to rename.)

  b Click . . . . **Rename...**

2 Type new name in . . . . **Name:** [ ]

3 Click . . . . `OK`

Move Sheets within a Workbook

Move One Sheet

- Drag . . . . ⎝ Sheet # ⟋
  (*Sheet #* is the name of sheet to move.)
  to . . . . *desired sheet tab position*
  Pointer becomes a ⬚, and black triangle indicates point of insertion.

Move Multiple Sheets

1 Select . . . . *sheets to move*
2 Drag . . . . *active (bold) sheet in group*
  to . . . . *desired sheet tab position*
  Pointer changes to ⬚, and black triangle indicates point of insertion.

Move Sheets to Another Workbook

NOTE: Excel will rename moved sheets when a sheet with the same name exists in the destination workbook.

1 Arrange . . . . *workspace*
  so both workbooks are in view.
2 Select . . . . *sheet(s) to move*
3 Drag . . . . *selected sheet(s)*
  to . . . . *a sheet tab position*
  in destination workbook.
  Pointer changes to ⬚ or ⬚, and black triangle indicates point of insertion.
  NOTE: If you drag sheets to an empty workspace area, Excel will create a new workbook for them.

Copy Sheets within a Workbook

NOTE: Excel will rename sheets that you copy.

Copy One Sheet

- Press <u>Ctrl</u> and drag . . . . ⟍ Sheet # ⟋
  (*Sheet #* is the name of sheet to copy.)
  to . . . . ***desired sheet tab position***
  Pointer changes to 🔄, and black triangle indicates point of insertion.

Copy Multiple Sheets

1 Select . . . . *sheets to copy*

2 Press <u>Ctrl</u> and drag . . . . *active (bold) sheet in group*
  to . . . . *desired sheet tab position*
  Pointer changes to 🔄, and black triangle indicates point of insertion.

Copy Sheets to Another Workbook

*NOTE: Excel will rename copied sheets when a sheet with the same name
exists in the destination workbook.*

1 Arrange . . . . ***workspace***
  so both workbooks are in view.

2 Select . . . . *sheet(s) to copy*

3 Press <u>Ctrl</u> and drag . . . . *selected sheet(s)*
  to . . . . *a sheet tab position*
  in destination workbook.
  *Pointer changes to 🔄 or 🔄, and black triangle indicates
  point of insertion.*
  *NOTE: If you drag sheets to an empty workspace area,
  Excel will create a new workbook for the sheets.*

Select Cells

(Also see Change Active Cell within Selection, page 53.)

Select One Cell

- Click . . . . **cell**

Select a Range of Cells

- Drag highlight through . . . . **adjacent cells**
  until desired cells are selected.

Select a Multiple Selection of Cells

1 Click . . . . **first cell**

2 Press <u>Ctrl</u> and click . . . . **each additional cell**
   AND/OR
   Press <u>Ctrl</u> and drag highlight through . . . . **adjacent cells**
   until desired cells are selected.

Select Entire Row or Column

- Click . . . . **row heading** or **column heading**

Select Adjacent Rows or Columns

- Point to . . . . . **first row heading** or **first column heading**
  <u>and</u> drag highlight through . . . . **adjacent headings**
  until desired rows or columns are selected.

Select All Cells in Worksheet

- Click . . . . **Select All button** ⬚
  located at intersection of row and column headings.

Deselect Any Cell Selection

- Click . . . . **any cell**

Select a Row or Column in Data Block

NOTE: A data block is a group of adjacent cells containing data.

1 Select . . . . **first cell(s) in block**

2 Point to . . . . **border of selected cell(s)**
   in direction to extend selection.
   Pointer becomes a ⬉.

3 Press <u>Shift</u> and double-click . . . . **selection border**

Continued ...

Select Cells (continued)

Select a Named Reference from the Name Box
*(Also see **Name Cell Reference**, pages 91 and 92.)*

• Select name in . . . . ***Name Box*** [＿＿＿＿＿｜▼]
  (The Name Box is located to left of the formula bar.)

Select a Cell Reference from the Name Box

1 Click in . . . . ***Name Box*** [＿＿＿＿＿｜▼]
  (The Name Box is located to left of the formula bar.)

2 Type . . . . ***cell reference***

3 Press . . . . [⏎]

  NOTE: *You can also select specific cells by selecting*
  Go To from the Edit menu.

Select (Go to) a Named or Specific Cell Reference

1 Press . . . . [F5]

2 Select reference name in . . . . **Go** to: *list*
  OR
  Type cell reference in . . . . **Reference:** [＿＿＿＿＿]

3 Click . . . . [OK]

Select Visible Cells Only

Selects cells crossing over hidden rows or columns without selecting the
hidden cells.

1 Select . . . . ***cells that cross over the hidden cells***

2 Click . . . . **Edit, Go To...**
  OR
  Press . . . . [F5]

3 Click . . . . [Special...]

4 Select . . . . ○ **Visible Cells Only**

5 Click . . . . [OK]

Select Cells Containing Special Contents

1 Select . . . . *any cell to search entire worksheet*

OR

Select . . . . *cells to search*

2 Click . . . . **Edit, Go To...**

OR

Press . . . . `F5`

3 Click . . . . `Special...`

4 Select . . . . *Select options:*
N̲otes, C̲onstants (N̲umbers, T̲ext, L̲ogicals, E̲rrors),
F̲ormulas (N̲umbers, T̲ext, L̲ogicals, E̲rrors), Blan̲ks,
Current R̲egion, Current A̲rray, Ro̲w Differences,
Column Differences, P̲recedents (D̲irect Only, All L̲evels),
D̲ependents (D̲irect Only, All L̲evels), Last Cell, V̲isible Cells Only, Ob̲jects

*NOTE: If Precedents or Dependents was selected,
Excel searches the entire worksheet.*

5 Click . . . . `OK`

Select (Find) Cells Containing Specific Data

1 Select . . . . *any cell to search entire worksheet*

or . . . . *cells to search*

or . . . . *sheets to search*
NOTE: Excel searches all sheets in a group selection, except modules.

2 Click . . . . **Edit, Find...**

3 Type characters to search for in . . . . . **Fin̲d What:** [   ]

NOTE: You may use wildcard characters (and ?)
to represent any character (?) or set of characters (*) in
the search criteria. To find data containing these special
characters, you must type a tilde (~) before the character.*

Continued ...

Select (Find) Cells Containing Specific Data (continued)

To specify a search direction:

- Select an option in . . . . **S̲earch:** [▼]
  Search options include: By Columns, By Rows,
  (All, Down, Up (module sheets only))

To look in specific places:

- Select an option in . . . . **Look in:** [▼]
  Look in options include: Formulas, Values, Notes,
  (Procedure, Module, All Modules, Selected Text (module sheets only))

To make search case specific:

- Select . . . . ☐ **Match C̲ase**

To find cells that match exactly:

- Select . . . . ☐ **Find Entire Cells O̲nly**

To find entire words, not characters that match:
(Module sheets only)

- Select . . . . ☐ **Find W̲hole Words Only**

To enable use of wildcards in search criteria:
(Module sheets only)

- Select . . . . ☐ **U̲se Pattern Matching**

4 Click . . . . [F̲ind Next]
Excel selects first cell meeting the search criteria.

5 Click . . . . [F̲ind Next]
to find next cell matching the search criteria.
NOTE: *You can reverse the search direction*
if you press Shift and click Find Next button.

6 Repeat step 5, as needed.

7 Click . . . . [Close]

52

Cell Selection Keys

To:	Press:
Select a single cell	⬆⬇
Extend selection in direction of arrow	Shift + ⬆⬇
Extend selection to beginning of row	Shift + Home
Extend selection to end of data block in direction of arrow	End , Shift + ⬆⬇
Select entire current row	Shift + Space
Select entire current column	Ctrl + Space
Select first cell in current row	Home
Select cell in current row in last occupied column	End , ⏎
Select first cell in worksheet	Ctrl + Home
Select last cell containing data in worksheet	Ctrl + End
Extend selection to first cell in worksheet	Ctrl + Shift + Home
Extend selection to last cell containing data in worksheet	Ctrl + Shift + End
Select entire worksheet	Ctrl + A
Select first or last cell in a horizontal data block* or select first or last cell in row	Ctrl + ← (first) or Ctrl + → (last)
Select first or last cell in a vertical data block* or select first or last cell in column	Ctrl + ↑ (first) or Ctrl + ↓ (last)
Extends selection to end of data block* in direction of arrow	Ctrl + Shift + ⬆⬇
Extend selection to include entire data block*	Ctrl + Shift + ✱
Extend selection up one screen	Shift + PgUp
Extend selection down one screen	Shift + PgDn
Deselect a multiple selection, except active cell	Shift + BkSp

A data block is a group of adjacent cells containing data.

Change Active Cell within Selection

NOTES: *In a selection, only one cell can be active. When a cell is active, you can enter data in the cell.*

- Select .... ***cell range***
  Excel activates first cell in selection.

To activate any cell using mouse:

- Press <u>Ctrl</u> and click .... ***cell to activate***

To move active cell from top to bottom:

- Press .... 🔲
  NOTE: *If selection is a single row,*
  moves active cell from left to right.

To move active cell from bottom to top:

- Press .... **Shift** + 🔲
  NOTE: *If selection is a single row,*
  moves active cell from right to left.

To move active cell from left to right:

- Press .... **Tab**
  NOTE: *If selection is a single column,*
  moves active cell from top to bottom.

To move active cell from right to left:

- Press .... **Shift** + **Tab**
  NOTE: *If selection is in a single column,*
  moves active cell from bottom to top.

To move active cell to next corner of selection:

- Press .... **Ctrl** + **.**

To move active cell to first cell in next range in a multiple selection:

- Press .... **Ctrl** + **Alt** + ➡

To move active cell to first cell in previous range in a multiple selection:

- Press .... **Ctrl** + **Alt** + ⬅

Enter Text

NOTE: Text entries cannot be calculated. By default, text is left-aligned.

1 Select . . . . **cell(s) to receive text**

2 Type . . . . **text**

   *NOTES: If what you type matches a previous entry in the current column, Excel's **AutoComplete** feature fills in text as you type. You can type over the suggested text or accept it by pressing Enter.*

   *If what you type has been set up as an **AutoCorrect** abbreviation (page 59), Excel replaces the abbreviation with the replacment text.*

3 Enter . . . . **⏎**

   *NOTE: To have the text wrap in one cell, see **Wrap Text in a Cell**, page 147.*

Enter Text by Picking from a List

Select text to enter in a cell from a list of entries you have made in the current column.

1 Right-click . . . . **cell to receive text**

2 Click . . . . **Pick from list...**

3 Click . . . . **desired entry in list**

Enter Numbers as Text

NOTE: Numbers entered as text cannot be calculated. By default, numbers entered as text are left-aligned.

1 Select . . . . **cell(s) to receive data**

2 Press . . . . **'**

3 Type . . . . **number**

   EXAMPLE: '1305

4 Enter . . . . **⏎**

Enter Numbers as Values

NOTE: Numbers can be calculated. By default, numbers are right-aligned.

1 Select . . . . *cell(s) to receive numbers*

To format the number as currency:

• Press . . . . **$**

2 Type . . . . *number*
   NOTE: Precede negative number with a minus sign (-),
   or enclose negative number within parentheses ().

To format the number as a percentage:

• Press . . . . **%**

3 Enter . . . . **⏎**
   NOTES: If Excel displays ######, column is not wide enough to
   *display the number. To change column width, see **Change Column***
   ***Widths**, page 142.*
   *To change the format, see **Format Number, Date or Time**, page 154.*

Enter Numbers as Fractions

NOTE: Numbers can be calculated. By default, numbers are right-aligned.

1 Select . . . . *cell(s) to receive numbers*

2 Type Zero **0**

3 Press . . . . **Space**

4 Type . . . . *fraction*
   Example: 0 1/4

5 Enter . . . . **⏎**
   NOTE: If Excel displays ######, column is not wide enough to
   *display the date. To change column width, see **Change Column***
   ***Widths**, page 142.*

Enter Mixed Numbers

NOTE: Numbers can be calculated. By default, numbers are right-aligned.

1 Select . . . . **cell(s) to receive numbers**

2 Type . . . . **number**

3 Press . . . . `Space`

4 Type . . . . **fraction**
Example: 5 1/4

5 Enter . . . . `⏎`

NOTE: If Excel displays ######, column is not wide enough to display the date. To change column width, see **Change Column Widths,** *page 142.*

Enter a Date

NOTE: A date entry is a number and is right-aligned.

1 Select . . . . **cell to receive date**

To enter current date:

* Press . . . . `Ctrl`+`;`

To enter a specific date:

* Type . . . . **date in valid format**
You may use the following formats:
m/d/yy   (e.g. 6/24/52)
d-mmm   (e.g. 24-Jun)
d-mmm-yy (e.g. 24-Jun-52)
mmm-yy   (e.g. Jun-52)

2 Enter . . . . `⏎`

NOTES: If Excel displays ######, column is not wide enough to display the date. To change column width, see **Change Column Widths,** *page 142.*
To change the format, see **Format Number, Date or Time,** *page 154.*

Enter a Time

NOTE: A time entry is a number and is right-aligned.

1 Select . . . . *cell to receive time*

To enter current time:

• Press . . . . **Ctrl** + **Shift** + **:**

To enter a specific time:

• Type . . . . *time in a valid format*

You may use the following formats:
h:mm:ss AM/PM	*(e.g. 1:55:25 PM)*
h:mm AM/PM	*(e.g. 1:55 PM)*
h:mm	*(e.g. 1:55)*
h:mm:ss	*(e.g. 1:55:25)*

2 Enter . . . . **⏎**

NOTES: If Excel displays ######, column is not wide enough to display the date. To change column width, see **Change Column Widths,** *page 142.*
To change the format, see **Format Number, Date or Time,** *page 154.*

Enter a Date and Time in One Cell

1 Select . . . . *cell to receive date and time*

2 Type . . . . *date in a valid format*
(m/d/yy – e.g. 6/24/52)

3 Press . . . . **Space**

4 Type . . . . *time in a valid format*
(h:mm – e.g. 1:55)

5 Enter . . . . **⏎**

Cancel a Cell Entry Before It is Entered

- Click . . . . **Cancel button** ☒
  on formula bar.

OR

- Press . . . . |Esc|

Enter Identical Data in Multiple Cells

1 Select . . . . **cells to receive data**
2 Type . . . . **data**
3 Press . . . . |Ctrl| + |↵|
  Excel enters data in all selected cells.

Enter Identical Data in Multiple Worksheets

1 Select (page 42) . . . . **sheets to receive data**
2 Type . . . . **data**
  Excel enters data in same cells in all worksheets in group.

Set AutoCorrect Options

1 Click .... <u>T</u>ools, <u>A</u>utoCorrect...

To enable correction of two consecutive capitals:
- Select .... ☐ Correct TWo INitial CApitals

To enable capitalization of names of days:
- Select .... ☐ Capitalize <u>N</u>ames of Days

To enable or disable automatic text replacement:
- Select or deselect ...... ☐ Replace <u>T</u>ext as You Type

To add an AutoCorrect abbreviation:
a Type abbreviation in .... <u>R</u>eplace: [   ]

b Type replacement text in .... <u>W</u>ith: [   ]

c Click .... [Add]

To delete an AutoCorrect abbreviation:
a Select abbreviation to delete in .... *list*

b Click .... [<u>D</u>elete]

To change an AutoCorrect abbreviation:
a Select abbreviation to change in .... *list*

b Type new replacement text in .... <u>W</u>ith: [   ]

c Click .... [<u>R</u>eplace]

2 Click .... [OK]

Set Excel to Add Decimal Places or Zeros Automatically

NOTE: This setting changes the values you enter in cells. To override this setting, type the decimal point when you enter a number.

1 Click . . . . **Tools, Options...**

> *FROM EDIT*

2 Select . . . . ☐ **Fixed Decimal**

3 Type or select number in . . . . **Places:** [⬍]

> *NOTE: The number you specify tells Excel to add decimal places or zeros to the numbers you enter in a worksheet.*
> *A positive number sets Excel to move decimal to the left.*
> *A negative number sets Excel to move decimal to the right (add zeros to value).*

4 Click . . . . [OK]

Set Edit Options

Sets defaults for entering, editing, copying, and moving data.

1 Click . . . . **Tools, Options...**

> *FROM EDIT*

2 Select or deselect . . . . *Settings options:*
> *Edit Directly in Cell – select to allow editing of data in cell.*
> *Allow Cell Drag and Drop – select to allow moving or copying cell contents*
> *by dragging and enable use of fill handle.*
> *Alert before Overwriting Cells – select to set Excel to ask for confirmation*
> *before overwriting data.*
> *Move Selection after Enter – select to move active cell (Down, Right, Up,*
> *Left) after you press Enter.*
> *Fixed Decimal Places – select to set Excel to add decimal places or zeros*
> *automatically (see above).*
> *Cut, Copy, and Sort Objects with Cells – select to keep objects with cells*
> *when you cut, copy, filter, or sort.*
> *Ask to Update Automatic Links – select to show link messages.*
> *Animate Insertion and Deletion – select to animate worksheet changes.*
> *Enable AutoComplete for Cell Values – select to enable this feature.*

3 Click . . . . [OK]

Enable Cell Editing

1 Double-click . . . . *cell to edit*
   OR
   a Select . . . . *cell to edit*
   b Press **F2**
   An insertion point appears in active cell and these buttons
   appear on formula bar:
   ☒ *Cancel button* – *cancels changes made in cell*
   ☑ *Enter button* – *accepts changes made in cell*
   fx *Function Wizard button* – *starts Function Wizard.*

   ### To edit the data in the formula bar:
   • Click . . . . *anywhere in formula bar*

2 Edit . . . . *data*
   Refer to the following procedures:
   Select Data to Edit, pages 61 and 62.
   Move Insertion Point in a Cell or Formula Bar, page 63.
   Edit Cell Contents (Options), page 64.
   Build a Formula, page 87.

3 Press . . . . **↵**
   to accept changes
   OR
   Press . . . . **Esc**
   to cancel changes.

Select Data to Edit ► Using Mouse

• Double-click . . . . *cell to edit*
   (Also see Enable Cell Editing, above.)

   ### To position insertion point:
   • Click . . . . *desired data position*

   ### To select a group of consecutive characters:
   • Drag . . . . *highlight over characters*

   ### To select a word or cell reference:
   • Double-click . . . . *word* or *cell reference*

Select Data to Edit ► Using Keyboard

1 Double-click . . . . ***cell to edit***
(Also see Enable Cell Editing, page 61.)

2 Press . . . . |⇅|
<u>until</u> insertion point is in desired position.

To select one character left or right:

● Press . . . . |Shift|+|⇆|

To extend selection one word left or right:

● Press . . . . |Ctrl|+|Shift|+|⇆|

To extend selection to beginning of line:

● Press . . . . |Shift|+|Home|

To extend selection to end of line:

● Press . . . . |Shift|+|End|

To extend selection to beginning of data entry:
When entry includes more than one line of data.

● Press . . . . |Ctrl|+|Shift|+|Home|

To extend selection to end of data entry:
When entry includes more than one line of data.

● Press . . . . |Ctrl|+|Shift|+|End|

Move Insertion Point in a Cell or Formula Bar ► Using Keyboard

• Double-click . . . . *cell to edit*
(Also see **Enable Cell Editing**, page 61.)

To move one character left or right:

• Press . . . . ⇄

To move one word left or right:

• Press . . . . Ctrl + ⇄

To move to beginning of line:

• Press . . . . Home

To move to end of line:

• Press . . . . End

To move to beginning of data entry:
When entry includes more than one line of data.

• Press . . . . Ctrl + Home

To move to end of data entry:
When entry includes more than one line of data.

• Press . . . . Ctrl + End

Edit Cell Contents (Options)

- Double-click . . . . ***cell to edit***
  *(Also see **Enable Cell Editing**, page 61.)*

To delete character to right of insertion point:

- Press . . . . `Del`

To delete character to left of insertion point:

- Press . . . . `BkSp`

To delete selected data:

- Press . . . . `Del`

To delete to end of line:
When entry includes more than one line of data.

- Press . . . . `Ctrl`+`Del`

To copy selected data to Clipboard:

- Click . . . . ***Copy button*** 📋
  on Standard toolbar.

  OR

  Press . . . . `Ctrl`+`C`

To delete selected data and transfer to Clipboard:

- Click . . . . ***Cut button*** ✂
  on Standard toolbar.

  OR

  Press . . . . `Ctrl`+`X`

To paste Clipboard data at insertion point:

- Click . . . . ***Paste button*** 📋
  on Standard toolbar.

  OR

  Press . . . . `Ctrl`+`V`

To insert a line break at insertion point:

- Press . . . . `Alt`+`⏎`

Move Cell Contents ▶ Using Toolbar

1 Select . . . . *cell(s) to move*

2 Click . . . . *Cut button* 🗡
on Standard toolbar.
A flashing outline surrounds selection.

To change destination workbook or worksheet:

- Select . . . . *workbook* and/or *sheet*

3 Select . . . . *destination cell(s)*
NOTE: Select an area the same shape as the area to move,
or select the upper left cell in the destination cell range.

To <u>overwrite</u> data in destination cells:

- Enter . . . . 🔲

To <u>insert</u> data between destination cells:

a Right-click . . . . *any destination cell*

b Click . . . . **Insert Cut Cells**

c If prompted, select . . . . *Insert Paste option:*
Shift Cells <u>R</u>ight, Shift Cells <u>D</u>own

d Click . . . . [OK]

Move Cell Contents ▶ by Dragging

1 Select . . . . *cell(s) to move*

2 Point to . . . . *any border of selected cells*
Pointer becomes a ⬉

NOTE: When dragging selection (see below), you can change
the destination worksheet, by pressing **Alt** and pointing to
the desired worksheet tab. To change destination workbook,
drag selection to desired workbook window.

To overwrite data in destination cells:

a Drag . . . . *border outline to new location*

b Click . . . . | OK |

To insert data between destination cells:

a Press Shift and drag . . . . *insertion outline*
   onto . . . . *row gridline* or *column gridline*

b Release . . . . *mouse button, then the key*

Move Cell Contents ▶ Using Menu

1 Select . . . . *cell(s) to move*

2 Click . . . . **Edit, Cut**
A flashing outline surrounds selection.

To change destination workbook or worksheet:

• Select . . . . *workbook* and/or *sheet*

3 Select . . . . *destination cell(s)*
NOTE: Select an area the same shape as the area to move,
or select the upper left cell in the destination cell range.

To overwrite data in destination cells:

• Enter . . . . ⏎

To insert data between destination cells:

a Click . . . . **Insert, Cut Cells**

b If prompted, select . . . . **Insert Paste option:**
   Shift Cells Right, Shift Cells Down

c Click . . . . | OK |

Move Cell Contents ▶
Using Shortcut Menu

1 Select . . . . *cell(s) to move*

2 Right-click . . . . *any cell in selection*

3 Click . . . . **Cut**
A flashing outline surrounds selection.

To change destination workbook or worksheet:

- Select . . . . *workbook* and/or *sheet*

4 Select . . . . *destination cell(s)*
*NOTE: Select an area the same shape as the area to move,
or select the upper left cell in the destination cell range.*

To overwrite data in destination cells:

- Enter . . . . ↵

To insert data between destination cells:

a Right-click . . . . *any destination cell*

b Click . . . . **Insert Cut Cells**

c If prompted, select . . . . *Insert Paste option:*
Shift Cells Right, Shift Cells Down

d Click . . . . | OK |

Move or Copy Cell Contents ▶
by Dragging with Right Mouse Button

1 Select . . . . *cell(s) to move or copy*

2 Point to . . . . *any border of selected cells*
Pointer becomes a ↖
*NOTE: When dragging selection (see below), you can change
the destination worksheet, by pressing **Alt** and pointing to
the desired worksheet tab. To change destination workbook, you can
drag selection to desired workbook window.*

3 Press right mouse button
and drag . . . . *border outline to new location*

Continued ...

Move or Copy Cell Contents ► by Dragging with Right Mouse Button (continued)

4 Select . . . . **shortcut menu option:**
Copy (overwrite), Move (overwrite), Copy Formats, Copy Values,
Shift Down and Copy, Shift Right and Copy, Shift Down and Move,
Shift Right and Move

Copy Cell Contents ► Using Toolbar

CAUTION: This copy procedure overwrites data in destination cells.

1 Select . . . . **cell(s) to copy**

2 Click . . . . **Copy button** 🖹
on Standard toolbar.
A flashing outline surrounds selection.

To change destination workbook or worksheet:

● Select . . . . **workbook** and/or **sheet**

3 Select . . . . **destination cell(s)**
NOTE: Select an area the same size as the area to copy,
or select the upper left cell in the destination cell range.
*To copy to multiple areas, press **Ctrl** and click upper left*
cell in each destination area.

To copy once:

● Enter . . . . 🔳

To copy with option to repeat copy:

a Click . . . . **Paste button** 🖹
on Standard toolbar.

To repeat copy:

1. Click . . . . **upper left cell in destination area**

2. Click . . . . **Paste button** 🖹

3. Repeat steps **1** and **2** for each copy to make.

b Press . . . . Esc
to end copying.

Copy Cell Contents ▶ Using Menu

1 Select . . . . *cell(s) to copy*

2 Click . . . . <u>E</u>dit, <u>C</u>opy
A flashing outline surrounds selection.

To change destination workbook or worksheet:

- Select . . . . *workbook* and/or *sheet*

3 Select . . . . *destination cell(s)*
*NOTE: Select an area the same size as the area to copy,
or select the upper left cell in the destination cell range.
To copy to multiple areas, press Ctrl and click upper left
cell in each destination area.*

To copy once and <u>overwrite</u> data in destination cells:

- Enter . . . . 🔲

To <u>overwrite</u> data in destination cells (with option to repeat copy):

a Click . . . . <u>E</u>dit, <u>P</u>aste
To repeat copy:

   1. Click . . . . *upper left cell in destination area*

   2. Click . . . . <u>E</u>dit, <u>P</u>aste

   3. Repeat steps 1 and 2 for each copy to make.

b Press . . . . Esc
to end copying.

To <u>insert</u> data between destination cells:

a Click . . . . <u>I</u>nsert, Copied Ce<u>l</u>ls

b If prompted, select . . . . *Insert Paste option:*
Shift Cells <u>R</u>ight, Shift Cells <u>D</u>own

c Click . . . . OK

d Press . . . . Esc
to end copying.

70

Copy Cell Contents ►
Using Shortcut Menu

1 Select .... *cell(s) to copy*

2 Right-click .... *any cell in selection*

3 Click .... **Copy**
A flashing outline surrounds selection.

To change destination workbook or worksheet:

• Select .... *workbook* and/or *sheet*

4 Select .... *destination cell(s)*
NOTE: *Select an area the same shape as the area to copy,
or select the upper left cell in the destination cell range.
To copy to multiple areas, press* **Ctrl** *and click upper left
cell in each destination area.*

To copy once and <u>overwrite</u> data in destination cells:

• Enter .... ⏎

To <u>overwrite</u> data in destination cells (with option to repeat copy):

a Right-click .... *any destination cell*

To repeat copy:

1. Click .... *upper left cell in destination area*

2. Click .... **Paste**

3. Repeat steps **1** and **2** for each copy to make.

b Press .... Esc
to end copying.

To <u>insert</u> data between destination cells:

a Right-click .... *any destination cell*

b Click .... **Insert Copied Cells**

c If prompted, select .... *Insert Paste option:*
Shift Cells <u>R</u>*ight, Shift Cells* <u>D</u>*own*

d Click .... | OK |

e Press .... Esc
to end copying.

Copy Cell Contents ▶ by Dragging

1 Select . . . . *cell(s) to copy*

2 Point to . . . . *any border of selected cells*
Pointer becomes a ☝

*NOTE: When dragging selection (see below), you can change
the destination worksheet, by pressing **Alt** and pointing to
the desired worksheet tab. To change destination workbook,
drag selection to desired workbook window.*

To <u>overwrite</u> data in destination cells:

a Press <u>Ctrl</u> and drag . . . . *border outline to new location*

b Release . . . . *mouse button, then the key*

To <u>insert</u> data between destination cells:

a Press <u>Ctrl+Shift</u> and drag . . . . *insertion outline*
onto . . . . *row gridline* or *column gridline*

b Release . . . . *mouse button, then the keys*

Copy and Fill Adjacent Cells ▶
Using Fill Handle

CAUTION: This procedure overwrites existing data in destination area.
*NOTE: If Excel recognizes a pattern (series) in the cells to copy, it
does not copy the data, but extends the pattern into the destination area.*

1 Select . . . . *cell(s) to copy*

2 Point to . . . . *fill handle*
(Small square in lower right corner of selection.)
Pointer becomes a ✛

*NOTE: To prevent a series from being extended,
you must press **Ctrl** while executing step 3.*

3 Drag . . . . ✛
to extend border over adjacent cells in rows or columns to fill.

*CAUTION: Dragging ✛ over selected cells will delete the data.
If you do this, you can click <u>Edit</u>, <u>Undo</u> Auto Fill to undelete the data.*

Fill Cells with Contents of Selected Cells ► Using Menu

Copies cell contents and formats from a specified side of selected cells into remaining part of selection.

CAUTION: This procedure overwrites existing data in destination cells.

- Select . . . . ***cell(s) to copy and destination cell(s)***

  NOTE: Destination cells must be in the same row or column as cells containing data to copy.

To fill rows below with data from the top row:

- Click . . . . **Edit, Fill ►, Down**

To fill columns to the right with data from the left column:

- Click . . . . **Edit, Fill ►, Right**

To fill rows above with data from bottom row:

- Click . . . . **Edit, Fill ►, Up**

To fill columns to the left with data from the right column:

- Click . . . . **Edit, Fill ►, Left**

Copy Specific Cell Contents

Copies formulas, values, formats, or notes.

1 Select . . . . *cell(s) to copy*

2 Click . . . . **Edit, Copy**

   OR

   a Right-click . . . . *any cell in selection*

   b Click . . . . **Copy**
   A flashing outline surrounds selection.

To change destination workbook or worksheet:

   • Select . . . . *workbook* and/or *sheet*

3 Select . . . . *destination cell(s)*
   NOTE: Select an area the same shape as the area to copy,
   or select the upper left cell in the destination cell range.
   To copy to multiple areas, press **Ctrl** *and click upper left*
   cell in each destination area.

4 Click . . . . **Edit, Paste Special...**

   OR

   a Right-click . . . . *any destination cell*

   b Click . . . . **Paste Special...**

5 Select . . . . *Paste option:*
   All, Formulas, Values, Formats, Notes, All Except Borders

6 Click . . . . | OK |

Copy Formulas or Values and Combine with Data in Destination Cells

1 Select . . . . *cell(s) to copy*

2 Click . . . . **Edit, Copy**

OR

  a Right-click . . . . *any cell in selection*

  b Click . . . . **Copy**

A flashing outline surrounds selection.

To change destination workbook or worksheet:

  • Select . . . . *workbook* and/or *sheet*

3 Select . . . . *destination cell(s)*

NOTE: Select an area the same shape as the area to copy, or select the upper left cell in the destination cell range. To copy to multiple areas, press Ctrl and click upper left cell in each destination area.

4 Click . . . . **Edit, Paste Special...**

OR

  a Right-click . . . . *any destination cell*

  b Click . . . . **Paste Special...**

5 Select . . . . ○ **Formulas** or ○ **Values** to set what type of data will be combined.

6 Select . . . . *Operation option:* to set how copied data will be combined.
None, Add, Subtract, Multiply, Divide

NOTE: Select None to overwrite existing data in the destination cells.

7 Click . . . . | OK |

8 Press . . . . |Esc|
to end copying.

Copy and Change Orientation of Data (Transpose)

Changes orientation of copied cells from rows to columns or from columns to rows.

1 Select . . . . *cell(s) to copy*

2 Click . . . . **Edit, Copy**

    OR

    a Right-click . . . . *any cell in selection*

    b Click . . . . **Copy**
    A flashing outline surrounds selection.

To change destination workbook or worksheet:

    • Select . . . . *workbook* and/or *sheet*

3 Select . . . . *upper left cell in destination area*

4 Click . . . . **Edit, Paste Special...**

    OR

    a Right-click . . . . *destination cell*

    b Click . . . . **Paste Special...**

5 Select . . . . ☐ **Transpose**

6 Click . . . . `OK`

7 Press . . . . `Esc`
    to end copying.

Copy Only Occupied Cells

Prevents any blank cells in cells to copy from overwriting data in the destination cells.

1 Select . . . . *cell(s) to copy*

2 Click . . . . **Edit, Copy**

OR

a Right-click . . . . *any cell in selection*

b Click . . . . **Copy**
A flashing outline surrounds selection.

To change destination workbook or worksheet:

• Select . . . . *workbook* and/or *sheet*

3 Select . . . . *destination cell(s)*
NOTE: Select an area the same shape as the area to copy,
or select the upper left cell in the destination cell range.

4 Click . . . . **Edit, Paste Special...**

OR

a Right-click . . . . *any destination cell*

b Click . . . . **Paste Special...**

5 Select . . . . ☐ **Skip Blanks**

6 Click . . . . │ OK │

7 Press . . . . **Esc**
to end copying.

Clear Cell Options ▶ Using Menu

Removes the formats, contents (data and formulas), notes, or all the above, and leaves the cells blank in the worksheet. References to cleared cells in formulas return a value of zero.

1 Select . . . . *cell(s) to clear*

2 Click . . . . **Edit, Clear** ▶

3 Select . . . . *Clear option:*
All, Formats, Contents, Notes

Clear Cell Contents

Removes the contents (data and formulas) and leaves the cells blank in the worksheet. References to cleared cells in formulas return a value of zero.

1 Select . . . . *cell(s) to clear*

2 Press . . . . Del

    OR

    a Right-click . . . . *any selected cell*

    b Click . . . . **Clear Contents**

Clear Cell Contents ▶ by Dragging

Removes the formats, contents (data and formulas), notes, or all the above, and leaves the cells blank in the worksheet. References to cleared cells in formulas return a value of zero.

1 Select . . . . *cell(s) to clear*

2 Point to . . . . *fill handle*
    Pointer becomes a ✛

    NOTE: *The fill handle is small square in lower right corner of a cell selection.*

To clear cell contents:

    • Drag . . . . ✛ *over selection*

To clear cell contents, formats, and notes:

    a Press <u>Ctrl</u> and drag . . . . ✛ *over selection*

    b Release . . . . *mouse button, then the key*

Delete Cells ▶ Using Menu

Removes the cells from the worksheet. Adjacent cells are shifted to close the space left by the deletion. If deleted cells have been used in a formula, the formula will show the #REF! error message.

1 Select . . . . ***cell(s) to delete***

2 Click . . . . **Edit, Delete...**

OR

a Right-click . . . . ***any cell in selection***

b Click . . . . **Delete...**

3 Select . . . . ***Delete option:***
Shift Cells Left, Shift Cells Up, Entire Row, Entire Column

4 Click . . . . | OK |

Delete Rows or Columns ▶
Using Menu

NOTE: Deleting removes the rows or columns from the worksheet and shifts adjacent rows or columns into the space left by the deletion. If cells in the deleted rows or columns have been used in a formula, the formula will show the #REF! error message.

1 Select . . . . ***rows or columns to delete***

2 Click . . . . **Edit, Delete**

OR

a Right-click . . . . ***any cell in selection***

b Click . . . . **Delete**

Delete Cells, Rows, or Columns ► by Dragging

Removes the cells, rows, or columns from the worksheet. Adjacent cells are shifted to close the space left by the deletion. If deleted cells have been used by a formula, the formula will show the #REF! error message.

1 Select . . . . *cell(s), row(s), or column(s) to delete*

2 Point to . . . . *fill handle*
    Pointer becomes a +

    NOTE: *The fill handle is a small square in the lower right corner of a cell selection. The fill handle for selected row or column is located in the lower right corner of the row or column heading.*

3 Press <u>Shift</u> and drag . . . . ⇕ or ◄╫► *over selection*

4 Release . . . . *mouse button, then the key*

Insert Blank Cells ► Using Menu

NOTE: *Existing data is shifted to make room for inserted cells. Excel adjusts references to shifted cells.*

1 Select . . . . *cell(s) where insertion will occur*
    NOTE: *Select the same number of cells as the blank cells to insert.*

2 Click . . . . Insert, Cells...
    OR

    a Right-click . . . . *any cell in selection*

    b Click . . . . Insert...

3 Select . . . . *Insert option:*
    Shift Cells <u>R</u>ight, Shift Cells <u>D</u>own, Entire <u>R</u>ow, Entire <u>C</u>olumn

4 Click . . . . | OK |

80

Insert Blank Rows or Columns ▸ Using Menu

NOTE: Existing data is shifted to make room for inserted columns or rows. Excel adjusts references to shifted cells.

1 Select ...... ***rows or columns where insertion will occur***
   NOTE: Select the number of rows or columns you want to insert.

2 Click .... **Insert, Rows** or **Insert, Columns**
   OR

   a Right-click .... ***any selected cell***

   b Click .... **Insert**

Insert Blank Cells, Rows, or Columns ▸ by Dragging

NOTE: Existing data is shifted to make room for inserted cells. Excel adjusts references to shifted cells.

1 Select .... ***cell(s)***
   above or to the left of where insertion will occur.
   NOTE: Select the number of cells you want to insert.

   OR

   Select .... ***row(s)*** or ***column(s)***
   where insertion will occur.
   NOTE: Select the number of rows or columns you want to insert.

2 Point to .... ***fill handle***
   Pointer becomes a ╋
   NOTE: The fill handle is a small square in the lower right corner of a cell selection. The fill handle for selected row or column is located in the lower right corner of the row or column heading.

3 Press Shift and drag ..... ⬍ or ◀▮▶ ***down or to the right***
   to extend border <u>outside</u> selection.

4 Release .... ***mouse button, then the key***

Fill Cells with a Series of Numbers, Dates, or Times ► Using Menu

1 Enter . . . . *first series value in a cell*
to base series on a single value.

OR

Enter . . . . *series values in consecutive cells*
to base series on multiple values.

2 Select . . . . . *cells containing series values <u>and</u> cells to fill*
NOTE: *Select adjacent cells in rows or columns to fill.*

3 Click . . . . **<u>E</u>dit, Fi<u>l</u>l ►, <u>S</u>eries...**

To change proposed direction of series:

● Select . . . . *Series in option:*
<u>R</u>ows, <u>C</u>olumns

To change proposed series type:

● Select . . . . *Type option:*
<u>L</u>inear – *to increase/decrease each value in series*
by number in Step Value text box.
<u>G</u>rowth – *to multiply each value in series by number in*
Step Value text box.
<u>D</u>ate – *to set increment by days, weekdays, months or years.*
Auto<u>F</u>ill – *to fill cells based on values in selection.*

If Date was selected,

● Select . . . . *Date Unit option:*
<u>D</u>ay, <u>W</u>eekday, <u>M</u>onth, <u>Y</u>ear

To change proposed step value:

● Type a number in . . . . **<u>S</u>tep Value:** [   ]

To set stop value for series:

● Type a number in . . . . **St<u>o</u>p Value:** [   ]

4 Click . . . . [OK]

Fill Cells with a Series ▶
by Dragging with Right Mouse Button

1 Enter . . . . *first series value in a cell*
to base series on a single value.

OR

Enter . . . . *series values in consecutive cells*
to base series on multiple values.

2 Select . . . . *cell(s) containing series values*

3 Point to . . . . *fill handle*
Pointer becomes a ┼

4 Press and hold . . . . *right mouse button*
Pointer becomes an ⤢
<u>and</u> drag . . . . *cell border*
in direction to extend series.
*NOTE: Drag border down, or to the right, to create an ascending
series. Drag border up, or to the left, to create a descending series.*

5 Select series option in . . . . *shortcut menu option:*
*Fill Series, Fill Formats, Fill Values, Fill Days, Fill Weekdays, Fill Months,
Fill Years, Series...*

If Series was selected,

• Follow steps below step **4** in Fill Cells with a Series of
   Numbers, Dates, or Times ▶ Using Menu, page 81.

Fill Cells with a Series of Numbers, Dates, or Times ► by Dragging

1 Enter . . . . *first series value in a cell*
to base series on a single value.

OR

Enter . . . . *series values in consecutive cells*
to base series on multiple values.

2 Select . . . . *cells containing series value(s)*

3 Point to . . . . *fill handle*
Pointer becomes a +

If series is based on a single number,

- Press <u>Ctrl</u> and drag . . . . + *over adjacent cells*
  to extend border in rows or columns to fill.

OR

- Drag . . . . + *over adjacent cells*
  to extend border in rows or columns to fill.

NOTE: *Drag* + *down or to the right to increase values, or drag* +
up or to the left to decrease values.

Spell Check

1 Select . . . . *any cell*
NOTE: *This selection spell checks all cells, headers, footers,
embedded charts, text boxes, cell notes, and text in buttons.*

or . . . . *cells to check*
or . . . . *sheets to check*
or . . . . *word* or *phrase* or *object to check*

2 Click . . . . *Spelling button* [ABC]
on Standard toolbar.

OR

Click . . . . <u>T</u>ools, <u>S</u>pelling...
*The Spelling dialog box appears and Excel shows the first word not
found in its dictionary above the Change <u>T</u>o text box.*

3 Select . . . . ☐ **Always Suggest**
to list suggested words for each word not found in dictionary.

Spell Check (continued)

To replace word not found in dictionary with suggested word:

a Type replacement word in . . . . **Change To:** [   ]

OR

Select word in . . . . **Suggestions:** *list*

b Click . . . . [Change]
to replace only current instance.

or . . . . [Change All]
to replace all instances.

or . . . . [AutoCorrect]
to replace word and add it to AutoCorrect list.

To undo last change:

● Click . . . . [Undo Last]

To skip word not found in dictionary:

● Click . . . . [Ignore]
to skip only current instance.

OR

Click . . . . [Ignore All]
to skip all instances.

To add word not found to current dictionary:

● Click . . . . [Add]

To ignore uppercase words:

● Select . . . . ☐ **Ignore UPPERCASE**

To end spell checking:

● Click . . . . [Cancel]

OR

Click . . . . [Close]

4 Click . . . . [OK]

Find and Replace Data

1 Select . . . . *any cell to search entire worksheet*

 or . . . . *cells to search*

 or . . . . *sheets to search*

 NOTE: *If you select sheets, Excel will search all sheets in a group except modules.*

2 Click . . . . **E̲dit, R̲eplace...**

3 Type characters to search for in . . . . . . **Fin̲d What:** ▢

 NOTE: *You may use wildcard characters (? and *) to represent any character (?) or set of characters (*) in the search criteria. To find data containing wildcard characters, type a tilde (~) before the characters.*

4 Type replacement characters in . . . . **R̲eplace with:** ▢

To set a search direction:

- Select an option in . . . . **S̲earch:** ▢ ▾

 Search options include: *By Columns, By Rows, (All, Down, Up (module sheets only))*

To make search case specific:

- Select . . . . ▢ **Match C̲ase**

To find cells that match exactly:

- Select . . . . ▢ **Find Entire Cells O̲nly**

To set module find and replace options:

- Select an option in . . . . **Look in:** ▢ ▾

 Look in options include: *Procedure, Module, All Modules, Selected Text*

- Select or deselect . . . . ▢ **Find W̲hole Words Only**

- Select or deselect . . . . ▢ **U̲se Pattern Matching**

5 Click . . . . [F̲ind Next]

 Excel selects first cell meeting the search criteria.

Continued ...

Find and Replace Data (continued)

6 Select . . . . ***one of the following:***

To globally replace cell contents:

- Click . . . . ⬚ Replace <u>A</u>ll ⬚

  Excel replaces all matches and returns you to normal operations.

To selectively replace cell contents:

a Click . . . . ⬚ <u>R</u>eplace ⬚

  to replace contents of active cell and find next match.

  OR

  Click . . . . ⬚ <u>F</u>ind Next ⬚

  to retain contents of active cell and find next match.

b Repeat step **a** for each item found.

c Click . . . . ⬚ Close ⬚

  to close Replace dialog box.

Type New Formula

1 Select . . . . *cell to receive formula*

2 Press . . . . 🔲
Equal sign appears in formula bar and cell.

3 Type . . . . *formula*
EXAMPLES: `=A1*(B2:B10)/2` `=SUM(A1:A10)*5`

NOTE: *For information about inserting references and functions into a formula, see* **Build a Formula**, *below.*

4 Enter . . . . 🔲

Build a Formula

Use these procedures to insert the following into a formula:

- *A cell reference from any workbook or worksheet.*
- *A named reference.*
- *A named formula.*
- *A function (using the Function Wizard).*

Insert a Cell Reference

1 If necessary, type or edit . . . . *formula*
(See **Type New Formula**, above, and **Enable Cell Editing**, page 61.)

2 Place . . . . *insertion point in formula*
where reference will be inserted.
NOTE: *If necessary, type preceding operator or left parenthesis [(].*

3 If necessary, select . . . . *workbook* and/or *sheet*
containing cells to reference.
NOTE: *When you select a cell in another workbook, Excel creates a link to that workbook.*

4 Select . . . . *cell or cell range to insert in formula*
Reference appears in formula bar and cell.

To extend selection to the same cells in other worksheets
(insert a 3-D reference):

- Press <u>Shift</u> and click . . *last worksheet tab to reference*

5 Type or build . . . . *remaining parts of formula*
OR
Enter . . . . 🔲

Continued ...

Build a Formula (continued)

Insert a <u>Named Reference</u> or <u>Named Formula</u>

1 If necessary, type or edit . . . . *formula*
(See **Type New Formula**, *page 87*, and **Enable Cell Editing**, *page 61*.)

2 Place . . . . *insertion point*
where named reference or named formula will be inserted.
NOTE: If necessary, type preceding operator or left parenthesis [(].

3 **a** Click . . . . **Insert, Name ►, Paste...**

   b Select reference or formula name in . . . **Paste Name:** *list*

   OR

   a Press F5 (Go to) . . . . `F5`

   b Select reference in . . . . **Go to:** *list*

4 Click . . . . `OK`

5 Type or build . . . . *remaining parts of formula*

   OR

   Enter . . . . `⏎`

Insert a <u>Worksheet Function</u> Using Function Wizard

*NOTE: You can also insert a function by selecting
Function from the Insert menu.*

1 If necessary, type or edit . . . . *formula*
(See **Type New Formula**, *page 87*, and **Enable Cell Editing**, *page 61*.)

2 Place . . . . *insertion point*
where function will be inserted.

3 Click . . . . `ƒ*`
on formula bar.

– FROM FUNCTION WIZARD – STEP 1 OF 2 –

4 Select a category in . . . . **Function Category:** *list*

5 Select a function in . . . . **Function Name:** *list*

6 Click . . . . `Next >`

Continued ...

Build a Formula (continued)

— FUNCTION WIZARD — STEP 2 OF 2 —

7 Type or insert arguments in . . . . ***argument boxes***

> **NOTE:** *An argument is data you supply to*
> *a function so it can perform its operation.*

> *Depending on the function, you enter the following kinds of data:*

> **numbers (constants)** *— you can type numbers (integers, fractions,*
> *mixed numbers, negative numbers) as you would in a cell.*
> **references** *— you can type or insert references (page 87).*
> **named references or formulas** *— you can type or insert named*
> *references or formulas (pages 87 and 88).*
> **functions** *— you can type a function or click* f_x *(to left of argument box)*
> *to insert a function into an argument (nest functions).*

> *The Function Wizard describes the current argument, indicates if*
> *the argument is required, and shows you the result of the values*
> *you have supplied.*

8 Click . . . . | Finish |

9 Type or build . . . . ***remaining parts of formula***

> **OR**

> Enter . . . . ⏎

Edit Worksheet Functions ▶
Using Function Wizard

1 Select . . . . *cell containing function(s)*
   NOTE: Do not double-click cell.

2 Click . . . . *Function Wizard button* $\boxed{f_*}$
   on Standard toolbar.

   OR

   Press . . . . $\boxed{\text{Shift}}$ + $\boxed{\text{F3}}$

3 Edit or add arguments in . . . . *argument boxes*

   *NOTE: An argument is data you supply to a function
   so it can perform its operation.*

   Depending on the function, you enter the following kinds of data:

   numbers (constants) *— you can type numbers (integers, fractions,
       mixed numbers, negative numbers) as you would in a cell.*
   references *— you can type or insert references (page 87).*
   named references or formulas *— you can type or insert named
       references or formulas (pages 87 and 88).*
   functions *— you can type a function or click $\boxed{f_*}$ (to left of argument box)
       to insert a function into an argument (nest functions).*

   *The Function Wizard describes the current argument, indicates if
   the argument is required, and shows you the result of the values
   you have supplied.*

   ### To edit next or previous function in cell:
   a Click . . . . $\boxed{\text{Next >}}$ or $\boxed{\text{< Back}}$

   b Edit or add arguments in . . . . *argument boxes*

   c Repeat steps **a** and **b**, as needed.

4 Click . . . . $\boxed{\underline{\text{Finish}}}$

Using Text in Titles to Name Cells

NOTE: *You must convert titles that are numbers to text. Excel converts date values to text automatically. Spaces in text are replaced with underscore characters in the reference name.*

1 Select . . . . *cells containing titles for names*
and extend . . . . *selection*
to include cells to name.

2 Click . . . . _I_nsert, _N_ame ▸, _C_reate...

3 Select . . . . *Create Names in option:*
_T_op Row, _L_eft Column, _B_ottom Row, _R_ight Column

4 Click . . . . [OK]

Name Cell Reference ▸ Using Menu

1 Select . . . . *cell(s) to name*

2 Click . . . . _I_nsert, _N_ame ▸, _D_efine...
OR
Press . . . . [Ctrl] + [F3]

3 Type a name in . . . . **Names in _W_orkbook:** [ ]
NOTE: *To create a sheet-level reference, precede reference name with the sheet name followed by an exclamation point (!).*
EXAMPLE: SHEET1!expenses

To change reference for the name:

a Click in . . . . **Refers to:** [ ]

b Delete entire reference (including equal sign).

c Select . . . . *cells in worksheet to reference*
NOTE: *To add cells to the reference, click in reference in _R_efers to box where new range will be added, press **Ctrl** and select cells in worksheet to add to reference.*

To add another named reference:

a Click . . . . [_A_dd]

b Type new name in . . . . **Names in _W_orkbook:** [ ]

c Change reference for the name (see above).

4 Click . . . . [OK]

Name Cell Reference ►
Using Name Box

1 Select . . . . *cell(s) to name*

2 Click in . . . . *Name box* [_____|▼]
on left side of formula bar.

3 Type . . . . *name for selected cell(s)*

4 Enter . . . . [⏎]

Name Formula or Value

1 Click . . . . <u>I</u>nsert, <u>N</u>ame ►, <u>D</u>efine...

OR

Press . . . . [**Ctrl**] + [**F3**]

2 Type a name in . . . . **Names in <u>W</u>orkbook:** [_____]

3 Click in . . . . **<u>R</u>efers to:** [_____]

4 Delete . . . . *existing reference*

*NOTE: By default, Excel enters cell reference
to selected cells in <u>R</u>efers to box.*

5 Type . . . . *formula* or *value*

*NOTE: Precede formula or value with an equal sign (=).
Formula may be pasted from the Clipboard. Cell references
may be entered in formula by selecting cells in worksheet.*

To add another named formula or value:

a Click . . . . [<u>Add</u>]

b Repeat steps **2-5.**

6 Click . . . . [OK]

Edit or View Named Cell Reference or Named Formula

1 Click . . . . **I**nsert, **N**ame ▸, **D**efine...

2 Select name to edit or view in . . . **Names in Workbook:** *list*
Reference or formula appears in Refers to text box.

To change the name:

a Type new name in . . . . **Names in Workbook:** [   ]

b Click . . . . [Add]

c Select old name in . . . . **Names in Workbook:** *list*

d Click . . . . [Delete]

To change reference for the name:

a Click in . . . . **Refers to:** [   ]

b Delete entire reference (including equal sign).

c Select . . . . **cells in worksheet to reference**
NOTE: To add a reference to an existing reference, click in Refers to box (place insertion point where new range will be added), press Ctrl, and select new cells in worksheet to add.

To change formula or value for the name:

a Click in . . . . **Refers to:** [   ]

b Edit . . . . **formula** or **value**
NOTE: Precede formula or value with an equal sign (=). Formula may be pasted from the Clipboard. Cell references may be entered in formula by selecting cells in worksheet.

3 Click . . . . [OK]

Paste List of All Defined Names

Pastes names and their assigned references or formulas into worksheet.

1 Select . . . . **upper left cell**
where list will be displayed.
CAUTION: The list will overwrite existing data in destination area.

2 Click . . . . **I**nsert, **N**ame ▸, **P**aste...

3 Click . . . . [Paste List]

Replace Cell References with Defined Names

Excel searches worksheet for references that have been given names (pages 91 and 92) and replaces the references with their names.

1 Select . . . . ***any cell***
to replace all references with names in worksheet.

OR

Select . . . . ***cells containing reference to replace***

2 Click . . . . **Insert, Name ▶, Apply...**

3 Select names in . . . . **Apply Names:** *list*

4 Select or deselect . . . . ***options:***
Ignore Relative/Absolute, Use Row and Column Names

To set other options:

a Click . . . . | Options >> |

b Select or deselect . . . . ***options:***
Omit Column Name if Same Column, Omit Row Name if Same Row, Name Order – Row Column, Column Row

5 Click . . . . | OK |

Delete Named Cell References or Named Formulas

NOTE: Excel will display #NAME? *error message in cells containing formulas referring to a deleted name.*

1 Click . . . . **Insert, Name ▶, Define...**

2 Select name to delete in . . . . **Names in Workbook:** *list*

3 Click . . . . | Delete |

4 Repeat steps **2** and **3**, as needed.

5 Click . . . . | OK |

Use AutoSum

1 Select . . . . ***cell(s) to receive sum(s)***
*NOTE: Select blank cell(s) below or to
the right of cells containing values to total.*

To automatically calculate grand totals:

*   Select . . . . ***cells to sum including subtotals***
    <u>and</u> . . . ***a blank row and/or column adjacent to range***

2 Click . . . . ***AutoSum button*** $\boxed{\Sigma}$
on Standard toolbar.

OR

Press . . . . $\boxed{\text{Alt}}$ + $\boxed{=}$

*Excel inserts =SUM( ) function in formula bar, and a
flashing outline may surround cells to be totaled.*

To change proposed range to total:

*   Select . . . . ***cells to total***

3 If necessary, press . . . . $\boxed{\hookleftarrow}$
to total the numbers.

AutoCalculate Values in Worksheet

Displays a calculated value for selected cells in worksheet.

*   Select . . . . ***cells to calculate***
    Excel displays result, such as Sum=25,
    on AutoCalculate area in status bar.

To change calculation method:

a Right-click . . . . ***AutoCalculate area***
on status bar.

b Click . . . . ***desired function:***
Average, Count, Count Nums, Max, Min, Sum
Excel displays result, such as Average=5,
on AutoCalculate area in status bar.

Set Calculation Options

1 Click .... <u>T</u>ools, <u>O</u>ptions...

> *FROM CALCULATION*

To set <u>worksheet</u> calculation options:

- Select .... ***Calculation option:***
  <u>A</u>utomatic, Automatic Except <u>T</u>ables, <u>M</u>anual

  If Manual,

  - Select or deselect .... ☐ **Recalc<u>u</u>late before Save**
    Deselect to reduce time it takes to save a workbook.

To set <u>current workbook</u> calculation options:

- Select or deselect .... ***Workbook options:***
  Update <u>R</u>emote References – *select to set Excel to calculate formulas containing references to other workbooks.*
  <u>P</u>recision as Displayed – *select to calculate values as displayed instead of how they are stored.*
  1904 <u>D</u>ate System – *select to set Excel to use Macintosh (1904) date system. Otherwise, Excel uses Windows (1900) date system.*
  Save External <u>L</u>ink Values – *select to reduce the time it takes to load a workbook containing links to other workbooks.*

To set goal seeking iteration limits or to resolve circular references:

a Select .... ☐ **<u>I</u>teration**

b Type a number in ..... **Maximum It<u>e</u>rations:** ☐

c Type number in .... **Maximum <u>C</u>hange:** ☐
  to set maximum change between iterations.

2 Enter .... ⏎

Calculate Only Active Worksheet (When Calculation is Set to Manual)

Also updates charts embedded in worksheet and open chart sheets linked to worksheet.

• Press .... `Shift`+`F9`

Calculate All Open Workbooks (When Calculation is Set to Manual)

Also updates all charts in open workbooks and calculates data tables when Calculation is set to Automatic Except Tables.

• Press .... `F9`

Replace All or Part of a Formula with Resulting Value

Permanently replaces the formula or part of the formula with its result.

1 Double-click .... ***cell containing formula to convert***

To replace part of a formula with its result:

• Select .... ***part of formula to convert***

2 Press .... `F9`

3 Enter .... `↵`
   to replace formula with its result.

   OR

   Press .... `Esc`
   to cancel.

Replace More than One Formula or an Array with Resulting Values

1 Select . . . . *cells containing formulas or entire array*

2 Click . . . . **Edit, Copy**

3 Select . . . . *destination cells*
   NOTE: *You can select the same cells or new cells.*

4 Click . . . . **Edit, Paste Special...**

5 Select . . . . ○ **Values**

6 Click . . . . | OK |

7 Press . . . . |Esc|
   to end procedure.

Create a Link between Workbooks

1 Open . . . . *workbooks to link*

2 Arrange . . . . *workspace*
   so both workbooks are in view.

3 Select . . . . *cell(s) to reference*
   in <u>source</u> workbook.

4 Click . . . . **Edit, Copy**

5 Select . . . . *cell(s) to receive link*
   in <u>destination</u> workbook.
   NOTE: *If referencing more than one cell,*
   select upper left cell in destination cell range.

To paste link as values:

a Click . . . . **Edit, Paste Special...**

b Click . . . . | Paste Link |

   NOTE: *If a reference includes more than one cell,*
   Excel creates a single array formula in destination cells.

To paste link as a picture:

• Press <u>Shift</u> and click . . . . . . **Edit, Paste Picture Link**

6 Press . . . . |Esc|
   to end procedure.

Insert an External Reference in a Formula

1 Open .... ***workbooks to link***

2 Arrange .... ***workspace***
so both workbooks are in view.

3 Select .... ***worksheet to receive formula***
in <u>dependent</u> workbook.

4 If necessary, type or edit .... ***formula***
(See Type New Formula, page 87, and Enable Cell Editing, page 61.)

5 Place .... ***insertion point in formula***
where reference will be inserted.
NOTE: If necessary, type preceding operator or left parenthesis [(].

6 Select .... ***cell(s) to reference***
in <u>source</u> workbook.
Excel adds external reference to formula.

7 Type or build .... ***remaining formula parts***
OR
Enter .... 🔲
to complete the formula.

*NOTE: You can also type an external reference using the following
special characters:*

- **Single quotation (')** — *encloses the path, filename and sheet-level
    name. If you omit the path, Excel will open a dialog box from
    which you can select the folder containing the target workbook.*
- **Square brackets ([ ])** — *encloses the workbook filename.*
- **Exclamation signs (!)** — *separates the sheet name from the
    cell reference.*

EXAMPLE: `'c:\excel\[sales.xls]sheet2'!$A$1`

Remove a Link between Workbooks

- Follow steps to Replace All or Part of a Formula with Resulting
  Value, page 97; or Replace More than One Formula or an Array
  with Resulting Values, page 98.

Manage Links (External References)

1 Open or select . . . . *dependent workbook*
(workbook containing external references.)

2 Click . . . . **Edit, Links...**
Excel lists all source workbooks for the dependent workbook.

To update values from source files:

a Select source file(s) in . . . . **Source File:** *list*

b Click . . . . [Update Now]

To open source files:

a Select source file(s) in . . . . **Source File:** *list*

b Click . . . . [Open Source]

To replace the source with another workbook:

a Select source file to replace in . . . . **Source File:** *list*

b Click . . . . [Change Source]

c Select new source file in Change Links dialog box.

d Click . . . . [OK]

To exit dialog and return to dependent workbook:

• Click . . . . [Close]

Save Linked Workbooks

NOTE: Saving the source workbook(s) prior to saving the dependent workbook ensures that the workbook names in the external references are current.

1 Select and save . . . . *source workbook(s)*
(workbooks supplying the external references.)

2 Select and save . . . . *dependent workbook*
(workbook containing external references.)
(See Save Active Workbook As, page 37, and Save Workbook Again, page 36.)

Create a One-Input Data Table

1 Enter .... *initial value*
in input cell (item A below).

2 Enter .... *series of substitution values*
in desired column or row (item B below).

3 Select .... *cell to receive formula*

If substitution values are in a <u>column</u>,

- Select .... *cell one position above and right*
of first substitution value (item C below).

If substitution values are in a <u>row</u>,

- Select .... *cell one position below and left*
of first substitution value.

4 Enter .... *formula*
that refers to input cell (item C below).

5 Select .... *data table range*
containing formula, substitution values, and cells
where results will be displayed (item D below).

6 Click .... **Data**, **T**able...

7 Specify reference to input cell:

If substitution values are in a <u>row</u>,

- Select (in worksheet) or type reference
to initial input cell in .... **R**ow Input Cell: [＿＿＿]

If substitution values are in a <u>column</u>,

- Select (in worksheet) or type reference (item A below)
to initial input cell in ..... **C**olumn Input Cell: [＿＿＿]

8 Click .... [OK]

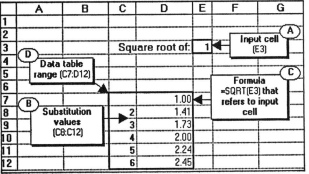

Create a Two-Input Data Table

NOTE: *An illustrated example with labeled items follows these steps.*

1 Enter . . . . ***initial value***
in row input cell (item A).

2 Enter . . . . ***initial value***
in column input cell (item B).

3 Enter . . . . ***series of substitution values***
in a column (item C).

4 Enter . . . . ***series of substitution values***
in a row (item C).
NOTE: *The first value in row and column are shared.*

5 Enter . . . . ***formula***
in cell containing shared substitution value (Item D.)
NOTE: *Formula must refer to row (item A)*
and column (item B) input cells.

6 Select . . . . ***data table range***
containing formula, substitution values, and
cells where results will be displayed (item E).

7 Click . . . . **D̲ata, T̲able...**

8 Select (in worksheet) or type reference
to row input cell in . . . . **R̲ow Input Cell:** [   ]
(Item A).

9 Select (in worksheet) or type reference
to column input cell in . . . . . . **C̲olumn Input Cell:** [   ]
(Item B).

10 Click . . . . [OK]

Create a Two-Input Data Table (continued)

Example of two-input data table:

	A	B	C	D	E	F	G	H	I	J
1								Row input		A
2	D							cell (E3)		
3		Area formula		Width:	1	◄				
4		=E3*E4 that refers	Height:	1	◄		Column input		B
5		to input cells					cell (E4)		
6									
7				1	2	3	4	5	6	Width
8	C			2	4	6	8	10	12	
9		Substitution		3	6	9	12	15	18	
10		values		4	8	12	16	20	24	
11		[C8:C13] and		5	10	15	20	25	30	
12		[D7:H7]		6	12	18	24	30	36	
13				7	14	21	28	35	42	
14	E			Ht.						
15		Data table								
16		range [C7:H13]								
17										

Add Substitution Input Values to a Data Table

1 Type .... *new substitution values* in cells adjacent to table.

2 Select .... *entire data table range* and extend .... *selection* to include new cells.

3 Follow steps **6-8** to create a one-input table, page 101.

   OR

   Follow steps **7-10** to create a two-input table, page 102.

Select an Entire
Data Table or Array

1 Select . . . . *any result cell*
in data table or array.

2 Press . . . . **Ctrl**+**/**

Clear an Entire Data Table or Array

1 Select . . . . *any result cell*
in data table or array.

2 Press . . . . **Ctrl**+**/**
to select entire range.

3 Press . . . . **Del**

Clear Results in a
Data Table or Array

1 Select . . . . *all cells containing results*
in data table or array.

2 Press . . . . **Del**

Calculate a Trend

1 Select . . . . *cells to receive trend values*
NOTE: *Include cells in a single column or row
containing existing values and additional cells, if desired.*

2 Click . . . . **Edit, Fill** ►, **Series...**

3 Select . . . . ☐ **Trend**

4 Select . . . . ◯ **Linear** or ◯ **Growth**

5 Click . . . . OK

Create a Lookup Table

Finds information located in a table:
- *VLOOKUP — compares values listed in a column.*
- *HLOOKUP — compares values listed in a row.*

NOTE: *An illustrated example with labeled items for VLOOKUP follows these steps.*

1 Enter . . . . **compare values**
in a column or row (item A).

2 Enter . . . . **data in cells**
adjacent to compare values (item B).

3 Enter . . . . **an initial compare value**
to find (item C).

4 Select . . . . **cell**
where result of lookup will appear (item D).

5 Press . . . . 🔳

6 Type function name . . . . **VLOOKUP** or **HLOOKUP**

7 Press . . . . 🔲

8 Select (in worksheet) or type . . . . **reference**
containing compare value to find (Item C).

9 Press . . . . 🔳

10 Select (in worksheet) or type . . . . **reference**
to entire lookup area (item E).

11 Press . . . . 🔳

12 Type . . . . **offset number**
representing the column offset (for VLOOKUP) or
row offset (for HLOOKUP) in table where data is located.

*EXAMPLE: Type a 2 if you want to show data
located in second column of table.*

13 Press . . . . 🔲

14 Click . . . . [OK]

Continued ...

Create a Lookup Table (continued)

Example of VLOOKUP table:

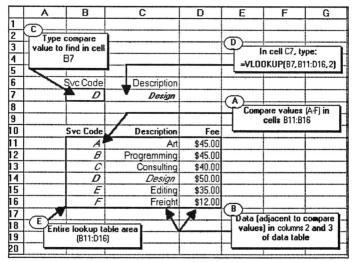

Consolidate Data ▶ by Category

Consolidate by category when your source data is <u>not</u> positioned in the same order on their respective worksheets and the source data uses identical category labels.

If data to consolidate is in separate workbooks,

- Open and arrange . . . . **workbooks**

1 Make sure source category labels are identical and consistently placed above or to the left of data.

2 Select . . . . **destination worksheet**

If destination worksheet contains outlining,

- Clear (page 139) . . . . **outline**

3 Select . . . . **upper left cell**
in area to receive consolidated data.
NOTE: This cell can be on a separate worksheet or on the same worksheet as the source data.

Continued ...

Consolidate Data ▸ by Category (continued)

4 Click . . . . **Data, Consolidate...**

5 Select a summary function in . . . . . **Function:** [▼]

To delete a source area reference:

a Select reference to delete in . . . . . . **All References:** *list*

b Click . . . . [Delete]

6 Select (in worksheet) or type
source area reference in . . . . **Reference:** [ ]
*IMPORTANT: Be sure the reference includes
the source category labels.*

7 Click . . . . [Add]
Excel enters reference in All References list.

8 Repeat steps **6** and **7** for each source reference to add.

9 Select . . . . ☐ **Top Row** or ☐ **Left Column**
NOTE: Excel will then use the labels to consolidate by category.

To ensure consolidated data remains current:

- Select . . . . ☐ **Create Links to Source Data**
  *NOTE: You cannot link the data if the destination
  range is on the same worksheet as the source data.*

10 Click . . . . [OK]

Consolidate Data ► by Position

Consolidate by position when your source data is positioned in the same order on their respective worksheets and the source data uses identical category labels.

If data to consolidate is in separate workbooks,

- Open and arrange . . . . **workbooks**

1 Make sure data to consolidate in source areas is arranged in the same order on their respective worksheets.

2 Select . . . . **destination worksheet**

If destination worksheet contains outlining,

- Clear (page 139) . . . . **outline**

3 Select . . . . **range to receive consolidated data**
NOTE: If you typed category labels in destination area, do not include them in selection. The destination range can be on a separate worksheet or on the same worksheet as the source data.

4 Click . . . . **D̲ata, Con̲solidate...**

5 Select a summary function in . . . . . **F̲unction:** [⬇]

To delete a source area reference:

a Select reference to delete in . . . . **All R̲eferences:** *list*

b Click . . . . [D̲elete]

6 Select (in worksheet) or type source area reference in . . . . **Reference:** [   ]
NOTE: Do not include source category labels in reference.

7 Click . . . . [A̲dd]
Excel enters reference in All R̲eferences list.

8 Repeat steps **6** and **7** for each source reference to add.

To create a link to the source data:

- Select . . . . ☐ **Create Links to S̲ource Data**
  NOTE: You cannot link the data if the destination range is on the same worksheet as the source data.

9 Click . . . . [OK]

Create an Array Formula

NOTE: An illustrated example with labeled items is provided below.

1 Type . . . . *values to be calculated*
by array formula in consecutive cells (item A).

2 Select . . . . *range of cells to receive array formula*
(the cells where results will appear (item B)).

3 Type . . . . *formula*
(Item C)
*NOTE: In the formula, be sure to specify entire
range of cells containing values to calculate
(such as the values 1 through 6 in the example).*

4 Press . . . . `Ctrl` + `Shift` + `⏎`
*Excel adds braces ({ }) to formula and displays resulting
values in each cell in array selection area (item B).*

Example of an array formula:

	A	B	C	D	E	F	G	
1								
2								
3			POINT/INCH CONVERSION TABLE					
4					C			
5						Type formula		
6			PTS	INCHES		=C7:C12/72		
7	A		1	0.013889				
8		Values	2	0.027778		then press		
9		calculated by	3	0.041667				
10		array formula	4	0.055556		CTRL+SHIFT+ENTER		
11		(C7:C12)	5	0.069444		(to create array formula)		
12			6	0.083333	B			
13						Array		
14						selection area		
15						(D7:D12) will		
16						display results		
17								

Edit an Array Formula

1 Double-click .... *any result cell in array*

2 Edit .... *formula as desired*

3 Press .... $\boxed{\text{Ctrl}}$ + $\boxed{\text{Shift}}$ + $\boxed{\hookleftarrow}$
Excel changes all formulas in array.

Extend an Array Formula to Include Additional Cells

1 Enter .... *new values for array formula*
to calculate in cells adjacent to existing array data.

2 Select .... *all cells in array*
<u>and</u> extend .... *selection*
to include new cells where results will appear.

3 Double-click .... *any result cell in array*

4 Edit .... *formula as desired*
NOTE: *In the formula, be sure to include reference
to cells containing new values to calculate.*

5 Press .... $\boxed{\text{Ctrl}}$ + $\boxed{\text{Shift}}$ + $\boxed{\hookleftarrow}$

Enter an Array Constant in an Array Formula

NOTE: *Use an array constant to specify multiple values in an array formula
instead of referring to values contained in the worksheet.*

1 Select .... *cells to receive array formula*

2 Type .... *formula*
in active cell of selection.

3 Place .... *insertion point*
in formula where array constant will be inserted.

Continued ...

Enter an Array Constant in an Array Formula (continued)

4 Type . . . . *array constant*
using option that matches the shape of your selection:

To type array constant for <u>single row</u>:

a Press . . . . **{**

b Type . . . . *numbers to calculate in #,#,# format*

c Press . . . . **}**

Formula example: ={1,2,3,4}*2
Result of example: 2 4 6 8

To type array constant for <u>single column</u>:

a Press . . . . **{**

b Type . . . . *numbers to calculate in #;#;# format*

c Press . . . . **}**

Formula example: ={2;3;4}*2
Result of example: 4

                          6

                          8

To type array constant for <u>row(s) and column(s)</u>:

a Press . . . . **{**

b Type . . *numbers to calculate in #,#,#;#,#,# format*

c Press . . . . **}**

Formula example: ={1,2;3,4}*2
Result of example: 2 4

                      6 8

NOTE: *Commas separate values in same row.*
Semicolons separate rows.

5 Complete formula, then press . . . . **Ctrl**+**Shift**+**↵**

Find a Specific Solution to a Formula (Goal Seek)

1 Enter . . . . *formula and dependent values*

2 Click . . . . **Tools, Goal Seek...**

3 Select (cell in worksheet) or type
reference to cell containing formula in . . . **Set cell:** [ ]

4 Type desired formula result value in . . . **To value:** [ ]

5 Select (cell in worksheet) or type reference to cell
containing value to change in . . **By changing cell:** [ ]

6 Click . . . . [OK]
Excel displays status of goal seeking.

7 If desired, select . . . . *Goal Seek Status options:*
Pause, Step, Continue

8 Click . . . . [OK]
to replace value in worksheet with solution value.
OR
Click . . . . [Cancel]
to retain original values.

Use Solver to Find the Best Answer

1 Enter . . . . *formula and dependent values*

2 Click . . . . **Tools, Solver...**
*NOTE: If Solver is not on the Tools menu,
see Install or Remove an Add-In, page 179.*

3 Select (in worksheet) or type
reference to target cell in . . . . . . **Set Target Cell:** [ ]
*NOTE: Target cell typically contains a formula referring
to cells that will change. If target cell does not contain
a formula, it must also be included as a changing cell (step 4).*

4 Select (in worksheet) or type
references to changing cells in . . **By Changing Cells:** [ ]
*NOTES: Type commas between references to non-adjacent cells.
Click the Guess button to have Solver propose changing cells.*

Continued ...

Use Solver to Find the Best Answer (continued)

To solve for a specific value:

a Select .... ◯ **Value of**

b Type target value in .... **Value of:** [   ]

To solve for a maximum or minimum target value:
(Requires you to set constraints)

• Select .... ◯ **Max** or ◯ **Min**

To add constraints:

a Click .... [Add]

b Select (in worksheet) or type reference
to cell to apply constraint to in .. **Cell Reference:** [   ]

c Select constraint operator in ..... **Constraint:** [▼]

d Specify constraint value in ...... **Constraint:** [   ]

   *NOTE: You can select (in worksheet) a reference in a
   cell containing the value or type a value or reference.*

   To add another constraint:

   1. Click .... [Add]

   2. Repeat steps **b-d**, as needed.

e Click .... [OK]

To change a constraint:

a Select constraint in .... **Subject to the Constraints:** *list*

b Click .... [Change...]

c Edit .... *constraint elements*

d Click .... [OK]

To delete a constraint:

a Select constraint in .... **Subject to the Constraints:** *list*

b Click .... [Delete]

Continued ...

114

Use Solver to Find the Best Answer (continued)

To set advanced options:

a Click . . . . | Options... |

b Select . . . . ***Solver options:***

Max Time – *limits time taken by Solver to find a solution.*
Iterations – *limits number of iterations used to find a solution.*
Precision – *sets precision for solutions.*
Tolerance – *sets percentage of error allowed in a solution.*
Assume Linear Model – *select to speed process in linear models.*
Show Iteration Results – *select to display results of each iteration.*
Use Automatic Scaling – *select to speed process when input and
        output values differ by large degrees.*
Estimates (Tangent, Quadratic) – *sets estimate process method.*
Derivatives (Forward, Central) – *sets derivative process method.*
Search (Newton, Conjugate) – *sets search direction for iterations.*
Load Model – *loads model settings saved with Save Model command.*
Save Model – *saves current model setting in worksheet.*

c Click . . . . | OK |

5 Click . . . . | Solve |

To create report(s) on a separate worksheet(s):

• Select report type(s) in . . . . **Reports:** *list*

To save problem for use with Scenario Manager:

a Click . . . . | Save Scenario... |

b Type scenario name in . . . . . . **Scenario Name:** | |

c Click . . . . | OK |

6 Select . . . . ○ **Keep Solver Solution**
OR
Select . . . . ○ **Restore Original Values**

NOTE: *You can restore original values and
still generate selected reports showing solutions.*

7 Click . . . . | OK |
to accept selected options.
OR
Click . . . . | Cancel |
to ignore settings and retain original values.

Create a Scenario

Scenarios are named sets of input values that quickly show different results in specified changing cells. There can be only one set of changing cells in a worksheet.

1 Enter . . . . *formula and initial values*

2 Click . . . . **Tools, Scenarios...**

> **NOTE:** *If Scenarios is not on the Tools menu, see Install or Remove an Add-In, page 179.*

3 Click . . . . | Add... |

4 Type name for scenario in . . . . . . **Scenario Name:** | |

5 Select (in worksheet) or type
references of changing cells in . . . **Changing Cells:** | |

To edit comment:

- Edit text in . . . . **Comment:** *list*

To set scenario protection options:

- Select or deselect . . . . **Protection options:**
  Prevent Changes – select to prevent others from making changes
  to scenario. (When Worksheet Protection is turned on.)
  Hide – select to prevent scenario name from being displayed in
  Scenario Manager dialog box. (When Worksheet Protection
  is turned on.)

6 Click . . . . | OK |

7 Type values in . . . . *each changing cell's* | |

To create another scenario:

a Click . . . . | Add |

b Repeat steps **4-7**, as needed.

8 Click . . . . | OK |

9 Select scenario to show in . . . . **Scenarios:** *list*

10 Click . . . . | Show |

11 If desired, repeat steps **9** and **10**.

12 Click . . . . | Close |

Use and Manage Scenarios

1 Click .... **Tools, Scenarios...**

To show a scenario:

a Select scenario to show in .... **Scenarios:** *list*

b Click .... | Show |

To edit a scenario:

a Select scenario to edit in .... **Scenarios:** *list*

b Click .... | Edit... |

c Follow steps **4-8** for **Create a Scenario**, page 115.

To delete a scenario:

a Select scenario to delete in .... **Scenarios:** *list*

b Click .... | Delete |

To merge scenarios:

a Click .... | Merge... |

b Select workbook name
containing saved scenario in .... **Book:** | ⬦ |

c Select sheet containing scenarios
to merge in .... **Sheet:** *list*

d Click .... | OK |

To create scenario report on separate worksheet:

a Click .... | Summary... |

b Select .... ◯ **Scenario Summary**

OR

Select .... ◯ **Scenario PivotTable**

If Scenario PivotTable,

• Select (in worksheet) or type
references to results cells in . **Result Cells:** | |
*NOTE: If you type references to non-adjacent cells,
type commas between each reference.*

c Click .... | OK |

2 Click .... | OK |

Create a Pivot Table

NOTE: *The illustration below shows how a pivot table could be used to evaluate categories of expenses in a list.*

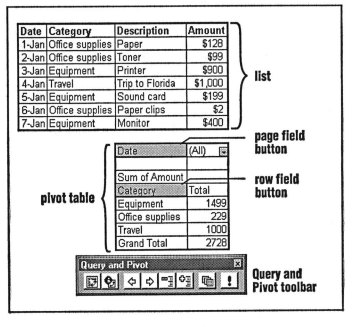

Date	Category	Description	Amount
1-Jan	Office supplies	Paper	$128
2-Jan	Office supplies	Toner	$99
3-Jan	Equipment	Printer	$900
4-Jan	Travel	Trip to Florida	$1,000
5-Jan	Equipment	Sound card	$199
6-Jan	Office supplies	Paper clips	$2
7-Jan	Equipment	Monitor	$400

list

page field button

Date	(All)

row field button

pivot table

Sum of Amount	
Category	Total
Equipment	1499
Office supplies	229
Travel	1000
Grand Total	2728

Query and Pivot

Query and Pivot toolbar

1 If evaluating a list, select . . . . ***any cell in list***

2 Click . . . . **D̲ata, P̲ivotTable...**
– *FROM PIVOTABLE WIZARD – STEP 1 OF 4 –*

3 Select . . . . ***Create PivotTable from data in option:***
Microsoft Excel List or Database, E̲xternal Data Source,
Multiple C̲onsolidation Ranges, A̲nother Pivot Table

4 Click . . . . | Next > |
– *FROM PIVOTABLE WIZARD – STEP 2 OF 4 –*

5 If necessary, select (in worksheet) or
type cell reference of data source in . . . . . **R̲ange:** | |
NOTE: *You can click Brow̲se, if the data source is external,*
then select file containing data to evaluate.

6 Click . . . . | Next > |

Continued ...

Create a Pivot Table (continued)

– FROM PIVOTABLE WIZARD – STEP 3 OF 4 –

7 Create . . . . *pivot table layout*

To add fields to pivot table:

*   Drag . . . . *field buttons*
    onto . . . . *a layout area*
    PAGE area – to let you display specific items for field in table.
    ROW area – to create row labels for each unique item in field.
    COLUMN area – to create column labels for each unique item in field.
    DATA area – to specify field to summarize.
    NOTE: *You must include at least one field in the Data area.*
    You can drag more than one field button into a layout area,
    but it's best to limit the number of fields when starting out.

To remove a field from pivot table:

*   Drag . . . . *field button off the layout area*

To move a field to another layout area:

*   Drag . . . . *field button onto desired layout area*

To modify how the field is used:

a Double-click . . . . *field button in layout area*

b Select (page 120, step 2) . . . . . *PivotTable Field options*

8 Click . . . . | Next > |

– FROM PIVOTABLE WIZARD – STEP 4 OF 4 –

9 Select (in worksheet) or type reference to upper-left
destination of table in . . . **PivotTable Starting Cell:** [ ]
NOTES: *If you leave this blank, Excel will create the pivot*
table on a new worksheet.
Do not place the pivot table where it can overwrite existing data.

10 If desired, type name in . . . . . **PivotTable Name:** [ ]

11 Select . . . . *PivotTable options:*
Grand Totals For Columns, Grand Totals For Rows,
Save Data With Table Layout, AutoFormat Table

12 Click . . . . | Finish |

Excel displays pivot table, and the Query and Pivot toolbar appears.

Modify a Pivot Table

1 Select .... *any cell in pivot table*

2 Click .... *PivotTable Wizard button* [⬚] on Query and Pivot toolbar.

OR

Click .... **Data, PivotTable...**

3 If desired, make changes .... *to field layout*

AND/OR

Click .... [Next >] or [< Back]

To change:	PivotTable Wizard	Page
Data source	Step 1	117
Reference to source data	Step 2	117
Fields in layout	Step 3	118
Pivot table position, Pivot table name	Step 4	118

Summary options – Grand Totals For Columns, Grand Totals For Rows, Save Data With Table Layout, AutoFormat Table.

4 Click .... [Finish]

Update a Pivot Table

Updates a pivot table to show changes made to source data.
NOTE: If rows or columns were removed or added to the source data range, you may have to follow the steps to modify a pivot table (page 119) and change the reference to the source data.

1 Select .... *any cell in pivot table*

2 Click .... *Refresh Data button* [!] on Query and Pivot toolbar.

OR

Click .... **Data, Refresh Data**

Modify a Pivot Table Field

Specifies how the pivot table will display or process the field data.

1   Double-click . . . . *desired field button in pivot table*

   OR

   – FROM PIVOTTABLE WIZARD – STEP 3 OF 4 –

   Double-click . . . . *desired field button in layout area*

   OR

   a   Select . . . . *desired item*
   in pivot table for field to modify.

   b   Click . . . . *PivotTable Field button*   [icon]
   on Query and Pivot toolbar.

2   Select . . . . *PivotTable Field options:*

   Data field options *(from PivotTable Wizard only):*
   Na̲me – to change field name.
   Summarize by – Sum, Count, Average, Max, Min, Product, Count Nums,
        StdDev, StdDevp, Var, Varp.
   Number – to format values in data field.
   O̲ptions – to specify a custom calculation to show data as: Normal,
        Difference From, % Of, % Difference From, Running Total in,
        % of row, % of column, % of total, Index.
   De̲lete – to delete field from pivot table.

   Row, Column, or Page field options:
   Na̲me – to change field name.
   Orientation – to change orientation of field to R̲ow, Column, or P̲age.
   Hide I̲tems – to select/deselect items to hide for field.
   De̲lete – to delete field from pivot table.
   Subtotals – A̲utomatic, C̲ustom, or N̲one.
            If C̲ustom, select Sum, Count, Average, Max, Min,
                Product, Count Nums, StdDev, StdDevp, Var, Varp.

3   Click . . . . `  OK  `

Move or Remove Fields on a Pivot Table ▸ by Dragging

- Drag . . . . *field button*
  onto . . . . *desired area in or off pivot table*

  NOTE: *Pointer indicates the result of the move as follows:*

  - *Move field to column* . . . . ▨
  - *Move field to row* . . . . ▤
  - *Move field to page* . . . . ◪
  - *Remove field from pivot table* . . . . ✖

Move Field Items in a Pivot Table

Changes position of an item and its related data within a field.
NOTE: *You can also sort (page 125) items in row or column fields.*

1 Select . . . . *cell containing item*

2 Point to . . . . *border of cell*
   Pointer becomes a ⤢

3 Drag . . . . *border outline to desired position in field*
   NOTE: *Excel will restrict movement to the field.*

Create a Group Field for Items in a Pivot Table

Groups items in fields to create a new field category containing the items you select. For example, you might group office supplies and equipment expense items to find totals for these items.

1 Select . . . . *items in a field(s) to combine*
   NOTE: *Selected items do not have to be adjacent.*

2 Click . . . . *Group button* ⮕
   on Query and Pivot toolbar.
   Excel creates a new field containing the grouped items.

Remove a Group Field in a Pivot Table

1 Select . . . . *any cell in grouped field*

2 Click . . . . *Ungroup button* ⬅
on Query and Pivot toolbar.

Modify a Group Field in a Pivot Table

(See Modify a Pivot Table Field, page 120.)

Group Date, Time or Numeric Items in a Pivot Table Field

1 Select . . . . . *cell in pivot table containing value to group*

2 Click . . . . *Group button* ➡
on Query and Pivot toolbar.

To change proposed start and end for group:

• Type values in . . **Starting at:** and **Ending at:** ▢

To change proposed interval for group:

• Select (for time or date) or
type (for numbers) an interval in . . . **By:** *list or text box*

If Days,

• Select or type number
of days in . . . . **Number of Days:** ▢⬍

3 Click . . . . ▢ OK

Undo Last Change to Pivot Table

• Click . . . . **Edit, Undo** . . .

Hide Details in a Pivot Table

NOTE: *You can double-click a <u>field item</u> to hide its details. Be careful not to double-click a <u>data field item</u> (usually a value); doing so will create a report on a separate worksheet displaying data for the item.*

1 Click .... ***a group item***
containing subordinate data to hide.

OR

Click .... ***a field button***
containing subordinate data to hide.

2 Click .... ***Hide Detail button***
on Query and Pivot toolbar.

OR

Click ..... <u>**D**</u>**ata,** <u>**G**</u>**roup and Outline** ▸, **H**ide Detail

Show Hidden Details in a Pivot Table

NOTE: *You can double-click a <u>field item</u> to show its details. Be careful not to double-click a <u>data field item</u> (usually a value); doing so will create a report on a separate worksheet displaying data for the item.*

1 Click .... ***group item***
containing hidden data to show.

OR

Click .... ***a field button***
containing hidden data to show.

2 Click .... ***Show Detail button***
on Query and Pivot toolbar.

OR

Click ..... <u>**D**</u>**ata,** <u>**G**</u>**roup and Outline** ▸, <u>**S**</u>**how Detail**

If no hidden details exist for field or item,

– FROM SHOW DETAIL DIALOG BOX –

• Double-click .... ***desired field name to show***

Display Specific Page Items in a Pivot Table

- Select item in . . . . *page field's* [_____ ▼]

Display All Page Items in a Pivot Table

- Select (All) in . . . . *page field's* [_____ ▼]

Create a Report for Each Page Field Item in a Pivot Table

Creates detailed reports on separate worksheets for all Page field items in a pivot table.

1 Select . . . . *any cell in pivot table*

2 Click . . . . *Show Pages button* [icon]
on Query and Pivot toolbar.

3 Select page field in . . . . <u>S</u>how All Pages of: *list*

4 Click . . . . [OK]
Excel inserts detail reports for each item on new worksheets.

Create a Report for a Specific Data Field Item in a Pivot Table

Creates a detailed report on a separate worksheet for a specific item in a pivot table.

- Double-click . . . . *desired data field item*
to create a report for that item.
*NOTE: A data field item is a value that
summarizes information in the pivot table.*
Excel inserts a detail report on new worksheet.

Sort Pivot Table Data

Also see Peform a Quick Sort, page 127.

1 Select . . . . *any item in field to sort*

2 Click . . . . **Data, Sort...**

To change proposed sort by cell:

- Select (in worksheet) or
  type reference to cell in . . . . **Sort by:** [   ]

To set the sort order:

- Select . . . . ◯ **Ascending** or ◯ **Descending**

To sort by values or alphabetically:

- Select . . . . ◯ **Values** or ◯ **Labels**

  *NOTE: To select Values, the Sort by cell reference (see above)
  must contain a value in the data area of the pivot table.*

To select a custom sort order:

a Click . . . . [Options...]

b Select an order in.... **First Key Sort Order:** [▼]

c Click . . . . [OK   ]

3 Click . . . . [OK   ]

Sort Data

1 Select . . . . *any cell in list*

OR

Select . . . . *range of cells to sort*

2 Click . . . . **Data, Sort...**

To set the first sort order:

a Select field, column, or row in . . **Sort By:** [_____ ▼]

b Select . . . . ◯ **Ascending** or ◯ **Descending**

To set second and third sort orders:

a Select field, column, or row in . . **Then By:** [_____ ▼]

b Select . . . . ◯ **Ascending** or ◯ **Descending**

To select a custom sort order first key:

a Click . . . . [Options...]

b Select an order in.... **First Key Sort Order:** [_____ ▼]

c Click . . . . [OK]

To specify a case sensitive sort order:

a Click . . . . [Options...]

b Select . . . . ☐ **Case Sensitive**

c Click . . . . [OK]

To change orientation of sort:

a Click . . . . [Options...]

b Select . . . . ◯ **Sort Left to Right**

c Click . . . . [OK]

To include or exclude header row:

• Select . . . . . ◯ **Header Row** or ◯ **No Header Row**

Continued ...

Sort Data (continued)

3 Click . . . . `OK`

> **NOTES:** *To sort by more than three columns, sort the list using the least important columns. Then, repeat the sort using the most important columns.*
>
> *When you sort rows that are part of an outline, Excel will keep outline families together.*
>
> *When you sort rows containing graphics, Excel will move the graphics with rows, if the graphics are set to move with the cell (page 190).*

Perform a Quick Sort

1 Select . . . . *cell in list to sort by*

or . . . . *range of cells to sort*
> **NOTE:** *The active cell determines the column Excel will sort by.*

or . . . . *item in pivot table field to sort by*

2 Click . . . . *Sort Ascending button* ⬛
on Standard toolbar.

OR

Click . . . . *Sort Descending button* ⬛
on Standard toolbar.

Undo a Sort

> **NOTE:** *To successfully undo a sort, undo it before carrying out other actions.*

• Click . . . . **Edit, Undo Sort**

Repeat a Sort

1 Select . . . . *cell(s) to sort*

2 Click . . . . **Edit, Repeat Sort**

Create or Edit Custom Lists

You can use a custom list to fill cells with a series and as a custom sort order.

1 Click . . . . **Tools, Options...**

FROM *CUSTOM LISTS*

To create a custom list:

a Select NEW LIST in . . . . **Custom Lists:** *list*

b Type list items in . . . . **List Entries:** *list*

  NOTE: *Items cannot begin with a number.*
  Enter items in the order you want Excel to
  use when creating a series or sorting a list.

c Click . . . . | Add |

To import a custom list from worksheet:

a Select (in worksheet) or
  type reference to cells
  containing list items in . . .**Import List from Cells:** | |

b Click . . . . | Import |

To edit a created custom list:

a Select list to edit in . . . . **Custom Lists:** *list*

b Edit list items in . . . . **List Entries:** *list*

To delete a created custom list:

a Select list to delete in . . . . **Custom Lists:** *list*

b Click . . . . | Delete |

c Click . . . . | OK |

2 Click . . . . | OK |

Lists

Excel automatically recognizes a labeled series of rows containing sets of data as a list. In a list, Excel treats rows as records and columns as fields. The field names are derived from the column labels.

Add Records to a List ▶
Using a Data Form

1 Select . . . . *any cell in list*

2 Click . . . . **Data, Form...**

3 Click . . . . `New`

4 Type data in each . . . . *record field* `        `

   NOTE: *Press Tab to move to next field. Do not press Enter after typing data in field, unless you want to add another record.*

To add additional records:

   • Repeat steps 3 and 4 for each record to add.

5 Click . . . . `Close`

Delete Records from a List ▶
Using a Data Form

Caution: Deleted records cannot be restored.

1 Select . . . . *any cell in list*

2 Click . . . . **Data, Form...**

3 Display (page 130) . . . . *record to delete*

4 Click . . . . `Delete`

5 Click . . . . `OK`

To delete additional records:

   • Repeat steps 3-5 for each record to delete.

6 Click . . . . `Close`

   Excel deletes record in list, and moves records up to close the space left by the deletion.

Display or Edit Records ▸
Using a Data Form

1 Select . . . . *any cell in list*

2 Click . . . . **D̲ata, F̲orm...**

To view next record:

- Click . . . . *down scroll arrow* ▼ or | Find N̲ext |

To view previous record:

- Click . . . . *up scroll arrow* ▲ or | Find P̲rev |

To scroll to a record:

- Drag . . . . *scroll box* ☐

To move forward ten records:

- Click . . . . *below scroll box*

To move back ten records:

- Click . . . . *above scroll box*

To edit displayed record:

- Edit data in each . . . . *record field* ☐
  to change.
  *NOTE: Press **Tab** to move to other fields, not **Enter**.*

To cancel changes made to current record:

- Click . . . . | R̲estore |
  NOTE: You must restore before moving to another record.

3 Click . . . . | Cl̲ose |

Find Specific Records ▶
Using a Data Form

1 Select . . . . *any cell in list*

2 Click . . . . **D̲ata, F̲orm...**

3 Click . . . . | Cr̲iteria |

4 Type a criterion for search in.. . . . . . *record field* | |

NOTE: *You may use wildcard characters (? and *) to represent any character (?) or set of characters (*) in a criterion. To find data containing a wildcard character, type a tilde (~) before the character.*

EXAMPLES:

> *Type* `pau` *in a character field to find records beginning with* `pau`, *such as* `Paul` *or* `Paula`.

> *Type* `>=1/1/89` *in a date field to find records containing dates on or after* `1/1/89`.

> *Type* `(718) ???-????` *In a character field to find phone numbers that have a* `718` *area code.*

> *Type* `* Shaw` *in a character field to find records that have any first name and* `Shaw` *as a last name.*

5 To add criteria to additional fields, repeat step **4**.

6 Click . . . . | Find N̲ext |

   OR

   Click . . . . | Find P̲rev |

7 Repeat step **6** for each matching record to find.

To access entire list:

   a Click . . . . | Cr̲iteria |

   b Click . . . . | C̲lear |

   c Click . . . . | F̲orm |

8 Click . . . . | Cl̲ose |
   to return to worksheet.

Filter a List Automatically

*NOTE: You can use AutoFilter with one list in a worksheet at a time;
the list (to be automatically filtered) must have column labels.*

1 Click . . . . **any cell in list**

2 Click . . . . **D̲ata, F̲ilter ▸, AutoF̲ilter**
Excel adds drop-down list arrows next to each column label.

3 Click . . . . ▾
of label containing data to display.

4 Select . . . . **item from list**
In addition to a specific item you can select:

 • *(All) — to remove filter criterion for a field.*
 • *(Top 10...) — to show top ten values for a numeric or date field.*
 • *(Blanks) — to show only records that have no data in the column.*
 • *(NonBlanks) — to show only records that have data in the column.*
 • *(Custom...) — to specify up to two comparison criteria for data
   in the column.*

If Custom was selected,

a Select a column item in first . . . . ▾

b Select desired operator for item in first . . . . ▾

  To specify another criteria for column:

  1. Select . . . . ○ **And** or ○ **Or**

  2. Select column item in second . . . . ▾

  3. Select desired operator for item in second . . . ▾

*NOTE: If you select criteria from more than one drop-down list,
Excel will show only records meeting all the criteria.*

End AutoFiltering

 • Click . . . . **D̲ata, F̲ilter ▸, ✓AutoF̲ilter**

Show All Records in a Filtered List

 • Click . . . . **D̲ata, F̲ilter ▸, S̲how All**

Filter a List with Advanced Filtering

NOTE: The list must have column labels.

1 Set up (pages 134 or 136) . . . . *criteria range*

2 Select . . . . *any cell in list*

3 Click . . . . **D**ata, **F**ilter ▸, **A**dvanced Filter...

To change proposed list range:

- Select (in worksheet) or
  type range to filter in . . . . **L**ist Range: [　　　]

4 Select (in worksheet)
or type criteria range in . . . . **C**riteria Range: [　　　]
NOTE: Include the comparison criteria column label(s) with the criteria.

5 Select . . . . ○ **F**ilter the List, in-place

OR

a Select . . . . ○ **C**opy to Another Location

b Select (in worksheet) or
type destination reference in . . . . . . Copy **t**o: [　　　]
*CAUTION: If you indicate a single cell, Excel will copy
the filtered results to cells below and to the right of the cell,
overwriting existing data without warning.*

To hide duplicate records:

- Select . . . . ☐ Unique **R**ecords Only

6 Click . . . . [OK]

Work with Lists Filtered In-Place

When a list is filtered in-place:
- *One or more drop-down arrows change color.*
- *The status line reports the number of records (rows) found.*
- *The row headings change color.*
- *You can use the following features to work with only the visible cells:
AutoFill, AutoSum, Chart, Clear, Copy, Delete, Format,
Print, Sort, Subtotal*

Set Up a Criteria Range (for Comparison Criteria)

Tells Excel how to filter a list, prior to using Advanced Filtering (page 133).
For example, you might want Excel to display only records (rows) that meet
*either criterion: Region is **North** or Sales greater than or equal to **20000**.*

Region	January
North	
	>20000

Comparison criteria labels

Criteria range

Region	January	February
North	10111	13400
South	22100	24050
East	13270	15670
West	10800	21500

List range

Region	January	February
North	10111	13400
South	22100	24050

Results copied to another location

1 If necessary, insert . . . . **blank rows**
above the list you want to filter.

2 Type or copy . . . . **desired column label(s)**
to blank rows above list, as shown above.
*These labels are called **comparison criteria labels** and must*
be identical to the labels in the list you want to filter.

GENERAL GUIDELINES FOR SETTING UP A CRITERIA RANGE:

• *Enter criteria below comparison criteria labels.*
• *The criteria range cannot contain empty columns.*
• *To show only records meeting all of the criteria in the criteria range,*
  enter criteria in the same row.
• *To show records meeting any of the criteria in the criteria range,*
  enter criteria in different rows.
• *To show records meeting different criteria for the same column,*
  set up duplicate comparison criteria labels.

3 Enter criteria . . . . **in row(s) below criteria labels**

Continued ...

Set Up a Criteria Range — For Comparison Criteria (continued)

To show only records (rows) matching a value, date, or text:

- Enter . . . . *text, number, date, or logical value* to find in column.

  *EXAMPLE: Below **Region**, type **North**.*

  NOTE: *When you enter text, Excel will find all items beginning with the text criteria. For example, if you enter **Sam**, Excel will include records such as **Samuel** and **Sammy**.*

Examples of criteria:

To find:	Examples
an exact text match	=*"=text to find"*
any character in a specific position	*Topic?*
consecutive characters in a specific position	*Sa*y*
an actual question mark, asterisk, or tilde (~)	*What is that~?*
a value greater than a specified number	*>1000*

To show items that compare to a specified value:

- Use one of the following comparison operators before a value, date, or text criteria.

    =   (equal to or matches)

    >   (greater than)

    <   (less than)

    >=   (greater than or equal to)

    <=   (less than or equal to)

    For example, enter >1000 below the January comparison criteria label to show only records containing values greater than 1000 for that column.

4 Filter (page 133) . . . . *list with Advanced Filtering* to show results of criteria.

Set Up a Criteria Range (for Computed Criteria)

*Tells Excel how to filter a list based on a calculation, prior to using
Advanced Filtering (page 133). The example below shows only records that
have January sales greater than the average sales for February.*

Criteria range {	**Jan Sales**		← **Label for computed criteria**
	FALSE		← **Formula =C9>AVERAGE($D$9:$D$12) evaluates to FALSE**

Region	January	February	
North	10111	13400	**List range (formula refers to values in range C9:D12)**
South	22100	24050	
East	13270	15670	
West	10800	21500	

Region	January	February	**Results copied to another location**
South	22100	24050	

1 If necessary, insert . . . . *blank rows*
above list to filter.

2 Type . . . . *label(s) for computed criteria*
in blank rows above list, as shown above.
Important: These labels must **not** match column labels in the list to filter.

GENERAL GUIDELINES FOR SETTING COMPUTED CRITERIA:

- *Enter criteria below labels for computed criteria.*
- *The criteria range cannot contain empty columns.*
- *To show only records meeting all of the criteria in the criteria range, enter criteria in the same row.*
- *To show records meeting any of the criteria in the criteria range, enter criteria in different rows.*
- *You can combine comparison (previous page) and calculated criteria to create complex conditions.*

3 Enter criteria
formula in . . . . . *row(s) below labels for computed criteria*

GUIDELINES FOR CRITERIA FORMULA:

- *Use a relative reference to point to the first value in column you want to evaluate.*
- *Use an absolute reference to indicate the column you want to compare.*
- *The formula must produce a logical (TRUE or FALSE) value.*
- *The formula must refer to at least one column in the list.*

4 Filter (page 133) . . . . *list with Advanced Filtering*

Subtotal a List Automatically

Creates subtotals for groups of data, and a grand total at the bottom of the list. Excel automatically applies outlining to the resulting list.
NOTE: *You can also do this to a filtered list.*

1 Sort (page 126) . . . . *column(s) in list to subtotal*
   NOTE: *List must contain labeled columns in its first row.*
   Items to subtotal should be grouped together.

2 Select . . . . *any cell in list*

3 Click . . . . **D̲ata, Su̲btotals...**

4 Select column label containing
   groups to subtotal in . . . **A̲t Each Change in:** [　　　　▼]

5 Select desired function in . . . . **U̲se Function:** [　　　　▼]

6 Select column label(s) containing
   values to calculate in . . . . **A̲dd Subtotal to:** *list*

To replace or retain current subtotals:

- Select or deselect . . . . . . ☐ **Replace C̲urrent Subtotals**

To force page breaks between subtotaled groups:

- Select . . . . ☐ **P̲age Break Between Groups**

To place subtotals and grand totals above data:

- Deselect . . . . ☑ **S̲ummary Below Data**

7 Click . . . . [　OK　]
   Excel inserts subtotals and outline tools appear.

Remove All Automatic Subtotals in a List

1 Select . . . . *any cell in subtotaled list*

2 Click . . . . **D̲ata, Su̲btotals...**

3 Click . . . . [　R̲emove All　]

Create Subtotals within a Subtotaled Group in a List

1 Sort (page 126) . . . . *columns in list to subtotal*

2 Subtotal (page 137) . . . . *first group in list*

3 Select . . . . *any cell in subtotaled list*

4 Click . . . . **D**ata, Su**b**totals...

5 Select column label containing next
group to subtotal in . . . . **A**t Each Change in: [▼]

6 Select desired function in . . . . **U**se Function: [▼]

7 Select column label(s) containing
values to calculate in . . . . **A**dd Subtotals to: *list*

8 Deselect . . . . ☑ **R**eplace **C**urrent Subtotals

9 Click . . . . [OK]

Work with a Subtotaled List

Excel automatically applies outlining to the subtotaled list. You can use the outlining level buttons to hide or show the details you want. You can then print or chart the results.
(See Show or Hide Outline Groups and Levels, page 141.)

Share a List on Network

1 Click . . . . **F**ile, S**h**ared Lists...

┌─────────── *FROM EDITING* ───────────┐

2 Select . . . . □ **A**llow Multi-User Editing

3 Click . . . . [OK]

4 Follow prompts to save the file.
NOTES: To update shared list with changes made by you and others, resave the file.
To show names of users working with shared list, select File, Shared Lists, then select Status tab.
*To track conflicts of data entries in shared list, select File, S**h**ared Lists, then select Show **C**onflict History from Editing Tab.*

Outline a Worksheet Automatically

NOTE: In the data to outline, references in formulas must consistently point in one direction (i.e., summary formulas in rows must consistently refer to detail cells above them).

1 Select . . . . *single cell to outline entire worksheet*

OR

Select . . . . *range of cells to outline*

2 Click . . . . **Data, Group and Outline ►, Auto Outline**
Excel creates an outline and displays outline symbols to the left of the row heading and/or above column headings.

Clear Entire Outline

1 Select . . . . *any cell in outline*

2 Click . . . . **Data, Group and Outline ►, Clear Outline**

Show or Hide Outline Symbols

1 Click . . . . **Tools, Options...**

FROM VIEW

2 Select or deselect . . . . ☐ **Outline Symbols**

3 Click . . . . | OK |

NOTE: To quickly show or hide outline symbols, press Ctrl+8.

Select an Outline Group

1 If necessary, show (see above) . . . . *outline symbols*

2 Press <u>Shift</u> and click . . . *desired show detail symbol* **⊞**
to select hidden group.

OR

Press <u>Shift</u> and click . . . . . *desired hide detail symbol* **⊟**
to select visible group.

Group Rows or Columns in an Outline

1 Select . . . . ***rows or columns to group***
NOTE: Select entire rows or columns containing detail data that is summarized by formulas below (for rows) or to the right (for columns).

2 Click . . . . <u>D</u>ata, <u>G</u>roup and Outline ▸, <u>G</u>roup...
If Group dialog box appears,

  a Select . . . . ○ <u>R</u>ows or ○ <u>C</u>olumns

  b Click . . . . | OK |
Excel displays outline symbols to the left of the row heading and/or above column headings.

Ungroup Rows or Columns in an Outline

1 Select (page 139) . . . . ***group in outline to ungroup***

2 Click . . . . . . <u>D</u>ata, <u>G</u>roup and Outline ▸, <u>U</u>ngroup...
If Ungroup dialog box appears,

  a Select . . . . ○ <u>R</u>ows or ○ <u>C</u>olumns

  b Click . . . . | OK |

Remove Group from Outline

1 Select (page 139) . . . . ***group in outline to remove***

2 Click . . . . <u>D</u>ata, <u>G</u>roup and Outline ▸, <u>C</u>lear Outline

Set Outline Options

1 Click . . . . . . <u>D</u>ata, <u>G</u>roup and Outline ▸, S<u>e</u>ttings...

2 Select or deselect . . . . ***Direction options:***
Summary rows <u>b</u>elow detail, Summary columns to <u>r</u>ight of detail

Continued ...

Set Outline Options (continued)

3 Select or deselect . . . . ☐ **A̲utomatic Styles**

4 Click . . . . [OK]

Show or Hide Outline Groups and Levels

*NOTES: If outline symbols are not visible, see **Show or Hide Outline Symbols**, page 139.*

You can also show or hide details using the S̲how Detail or H̲ide Detail command on the D̲ata, G̲roup and Outline menu.

Show Group Details

● Click . . . . *show detail symbol* ⊞
  of group to expand.

Hide Group Details

● Click . . . . *hide detail symbol* ⊟
  of group to hide.

Show or Hide All Outline Groups for a Level

● Click . . . . *row or column level symbol*
  for lowest level to show.

Select Only Visible Cells in Outline

Use this procedure to quickly format, chart, move or copy only the visible cells in an outline.

1 If necessary, hide groups or levels that are not to be selected (page 141).

2 Select . . . . *desired cells in outline*

3 Click . . . . **E̲dit, G̲o To...**

4 Click . . . . [S̲pecial...]

5 Select . . . . ○ **V̲isible Cells Only**

6 Click . . . . [OK]

Change Column Widths

One Column

1 Point to . . . . *right border of column heading*
Pointer becomes a ⟷

2 Drag . . . . ⟷ *left or right*
Excel displays column width on left side of formula bar.

Multiple Columns

1 Select . . . . *columns*
NOTE: *Click Select All button* ⬜ *to change all columns.*

2 Point to . . . . . *right border of any selected column heading*
Pointer becomes a ⟷

3 Drag . . . . ⟷ *left or right*
Excel displays column width on left side of formula bar.

Column to Fit Longest Entry

• Double-click . . . . *right border of the column's heading*

Column to Specific Size

1 Select . . . . *a cell in each column to size*

2 Click . . . . **F̲ormat, C̲olumn ▶, W̲idth...**

3 Type number (0-255) in . . . . **C̲olumn Width:** ☐
NOTE: *Number represents number of characters that
can be displayed in cell using the standard font.*

4 Click . . . . ☐ OK

Set Standard Column Width

*Changes column widths that have not been previously adjusted in selected
worksheet(s).*

1 Click . . . . **F̲ormat, C̲olumn ▶, S̲tandard Width...**

2 Type new number in . . . . . **S̲tandard Column Width:** ☐
NOTE: *Number represents number of characters that
can be displayed in cell using the standard font.*

3 Click . . . . ☐ OK

Reset Columns to the Standard Column Width

1 Select .... *column(s)*
NOTE: *Click Select All button* ⬜ *to reset all columns.*

2 Click .... **F**o**rmat, **C**olumn ▸, **S**tandard Width...

3 Click .... | OK |

Change Row Heights

One Row

1 Point to .... *bottom border of row heading*
Pointer becomes a ⇳

2 Drag .... ⇳ *up or down*
Excel displays row height on left side of formula bar.

Multiple Rows

1 Select .... *rows*
NOTE: *Click Select All button* ⬜ *to change all rows.*

2 Point to ...... *bottom border of any selected row heading*
Pointer becomes a ⇳

3 Drag .... ⇳ *up or down*
Excel displays row height on left side of formula bar.

Row to Fit Tallest Entry

• Double-click .... *bottom border of the row's heading*

Row to Specific Size

1 Select .... *a cell in each row to size*

2 Click .... **F**o**rmat, **R**ow ▸, **H**eight...

3 Type number (0-409) in .... **R**ow Height: [   ]
NOTE: *Number represents height in points.*

4 Click .... | OK |

Hide Columns ► by Dragging

One Column

1 Point to . . . . *right border of column heading*
Pointer becomes a ◄╫►

2 Drag . . . . ◄╫► *left*
to column's left border.
Excel displays a bolded column heading border where a column is hidden.

Multiple Columns

1 Select . . . . *columns*

2 Point to . . . . . *right border of any selected column heading*
Pointer becomes a ◄╫►

3 Drag . . . . ◄╫► *left*
to column's left border.
Excel displays a bolded column heading border where a column is hidden.

Hide Columns ► Using Menu

1 Select . . . . *a cell in each column to hide*
2 Click . . . . **F**ormat, **C**olumn ►, **H**ide
Excel displays a bolded column heading border where a column is hidden.

Show Hidden Columns ► by Dragging

1 Point . . . . *just right of bolded column heading border*
Pointer becomes a ◄╫►

2 Drag . . . . ◄╫► *right*

Show Hidden Columns ► Using Menu

1 Select . . . . *surrounding columns*
NOTE: Click Select All button ▭ *to unhide all columns.*

2 Click . . . . **F**ormat, **C**olumn ►, **U**nhide

Hide Rows ▸ by Dragging

One Row

1 Point to . . . . *bottom border of row heading*
Pointer becomes a ⇳

2 Drag . . . . ⇳ *up*
to row's top border.
Excel displays a bolded row heading border where a row is hidden.

Multiple Rows

1 Select . . . . *rows*

2 Point to . . . . . . *bottom border of any selected row heading*
Pointer becomes a ⇳

3 Drag . . . . ⇳ *up*
to row's top border.
Excel displays a bolded row heading border where a row is hidden.

Hide Rows ▸ Using Menu

1 Select . . . . *a cell in each row to hide*

2 Click . . . . **F̲ormat, R̲ow ▸, H̲ide**
Excel displays a bolded row heading border where a row is hidden.

Show Hidden Rows ▸ by Dragging

1 Point . . . . *just below bolded row heading border*
Pointer becomes a ⇳

2 Drag . . . . ⇳ *down*

Show Hidden Rows ▸ Using Menu

1 Select . . . . *surrounding rows*
NOTE: Click Select All button ☐ to unhide all rows.

2 Click . . . . **F̲ormat, R̲ow ▸, U̲nhide**

Align Data in Cells ► Using Toolbar

1 Select . . . . ***cell(s) containing data***

– FROM FORMATTING TOOLBAR –

2 Click . . . . ***Align Left button*** ▤

   OR

   Click . . . . ***Center button*** ▤

   OR

   Click . . . . ***Align Right button*** ▤

Align Data in Cells ► Using Menu

Aligns data horizontally or vertically in their cells.

1 Select . . . . ***cell(s) containing data***

2 Click . . . . **Fo̲rmat, Ce̲lls...**

   OR

   a Right-click . . . . ***any selected cell***

   b Click . . . . **Format Cells...**

---

*FROM **ALIGNMENT***

To align data horizontally:

● Select . . . . ***Horizontal option:***
   G̲eneral *(default alignment),*
   L̲eft, C̲enter, R̲ight,
   F̲ill *(cell appears filled with its contents),*
   J̲ustify *(aligns wrapped text right and left),*
   Center a̲cross selection

To align data vertically:

● Select . . . . ***Vertical option:***
   T̲op, C̲enter, B̲ottom,
   Ju̲stify *(aligns and wraps text evenly within its vertical limits)*

3 Click . . . . | OK |

Wrap Text in a Cell

Wraps text to fit in cell. The row height changes to accommodate the text, unless the row height was previously set.

1 Select . . . . *cell(s) containing text*

2 Click . . . . **F**o**rmat, C**e**lls...**

  OR

  a Right-click . . . . *any selected cell*

  b Click . . . . **Format Cells...**

  ┌─── *FROM ALIGNMENT* ───┐

3 Select . . . . ☐ **W**rap Text

4 Click . . . . [OK]

Justify Text in Cells

Justifies text to fit evenly within border(s) of cell. It wraps text, if text has not been wrapped before.

1 Select . . . . *cell(s) containing text*

2 Click . . . . **F**o**rmat, C**e**lls...**

  OR

  a Right-click . . . . *any selected cell*

  b Click . . . . **Format Cells...**

  ┌─── *FROM ALIGNMENT* ───┐

3 Select . . . . ◯ **J**ustify
  in Horizontal group.

  AND/OR

  Select . . . . ◯ **J**ustify
  in Vertical group.

4 Click . . . . [OK]

Justify Text to Fill a Range

Splits lengthy text to fit evenly in selected cells.

1 Select . . . . ***cell or consecutive cells in one column***
and extend selection <u>down</u> to include . . ***range of empty cells***
in which text will be distributed.

2 Click . . . . **E̲dit, Fi̲ll ▸, J̲ustify**

If prompted,

* Click . . . . [OK]
to extend text below selection.
Excel divides text evenly among selected cells.

Center Data Across Columns

Centers data in left-most cells of a selection, across blank cells to the right.
The centered data will remain in original cell(s).

1 Select . . . . ***cell(s) in a column***
and extend selection <u>right</u> to include . . ***range of empty cells***
in which data will be centered.

2 Click . . . . ***Center Across Columns button*** 🔲
Excel centers the data across selection of blank cells.

Change Orientation of Data in Cells

1 Select . . . . ***cell(s) containing data***
2 Click . . . . **F̲ormat, Ce̲lls...**

OR

a Right-click . . . . ***any selected cell***
b Click . . . . **Format Cells...**

┌─── *FROM ALIGNMENT* ───┐

3 Select . . . . ***Orie̲ntation option***
4 Click . . . . [OK]

Change Font ▶ Using Toolbar

1 Select . . . . *cells* or *characters in cells*

2 Select desired font in . . . . *Font* [▾]
on Formatting toolbar.

Change Font Size ▶ Using Toolbar

1 Select . . . . *cells* or *characters in cells*

2 Enter or select a number in . . . . *Font Size* [▾]
on Formatting toolbar.

Change Font Color ▶ Using Toolbar

1 Select . . . . *cells* or *characters in cells*

2 Click . . . . *displayed Font Color option* [🔲▾]
to apply it to selection.

OR

a Click . . . . *Font Color drop-down arrow* [🔲▾]
Excel displays a color palette.
NOTE: *To keep the color palette open,*
point to border of palette and drag it off toolbar.

b Click . . . . *desired color on palette*

Change Font ► Using Menu

1 Select . . . . *cells* or *characters in cells*

2 Click . . . . **Format, Cells...**

   OR

   a Right-click . . . . *any selected cell*

   b Click . . . . **Format Cells...**

┌──── *FROM FONT* ────┐

To change <u>font</u>:

- Select a font name in . . . . **Font:** *list*

To change font <u>style</u>:

- Select a font style in . . . . **Font Style:** *list*
  Font Style list items include: Regular, Italic, Bold, Bold Italic

To change font <u>size</u>:

- Type a point size in . . . . **Size:** [   ]

   OR

   Select a point size in . . . . **Size:** *list*

To select an <u>underline</u> style:

- Select an underline style in . . . **Underline:** [▼]
  None, Single, Double, Single Accounting, Double Accounting

To apply <u>special</u> effects:

- Select . . . . *Effects options:*
  *Strike**t**hrough, Super**s**cript, Su**b**script*

To set font to <u>normal</u> font style:

- Select . . . . ☐ **Normal Font**

To set font <u>color</u>:

- Select a color in . . . . **Color** [▼]

3 Click . . . . [OK]

Bold, Italicize, or Underline Text ▶
Using Toolbar

1 Select . . . . *cells* or *characters in cells*
– FROM FORMATTING TOOLBAR –

2 Click . . . . *Bold button* | **B** |
OR
Click . . . . *Italic button* | *I* |
OR
Click . . . . *Underline button* | U |

To remove font style:
• Click . . . . *format button again*

Apply Borders to Cells ▶
Using Toolbar

1 Select . . . . *cell(s)*
2 Click . . . . *displayed Border option* | ⬚ ⬇ |
to apply it to selected cells.
OR

a Click . . . . *Border drop-down arrow* | ⬚ ⬇ |
Excel displays a border palette.
NOTE: *To keep the border palette open,*
point to border of palette and drag it off toolbar.

b Click . . . . *desired border on palette*

Apply Custom Borders to Cells

1 Select . . . . *cell(s)*

2 Click . . . . **Fo̲rmat, Ce̲lls...**

OR

   a Right-click . . . . *any selected cell*

   b Click . . . . **Format Cells...**

FROM BORDER

3 Select a style for border in . . . . *Sty̲le group*

4 Select border to apply style to in . . . . *Border group*
   O̲utline, Left, R̲ight, T̲op, B̲ottom

To remove border:

   • Click border to remove in . . . . *Border group*

To change color of selected border:

   • Select desired color in . . . . **C̲olor:** | ▾ |

5 Repeat steps **3** and **4** for each border.

6 Click . . . . | OK |

Remove Borders from Cells

• Select . . . . *cells with borders to remove*

To remove all borders:

   • Press . . . . **Ctrl** + **Shift** + **−**

To remove specific borders:

   a Click . . . . **Fo̲rmat, Ce̲lls...**

FROM BORDER

   b Click border to remove in . . . . *Border group*
      until style is removed.

   c Click . . . . | OK |

Apply Color to Cells ▸ Using Toolbar

1 Select . . . . *cell(s)*

2 Click . . . . *displayed Color option*
to apply it to selection.

OR

  a Click . . . . *Color drop-down arrow*
    Excel displays a color palette.
    NOTE: *To keep the color palette open,
    point to border of palette and drag it off toolbar.*

  b Click . . . . *desired color on palette*

Apply Color or Pattern
to Cells ▸ Using Menu

1 Select . . . . *cell(s)*

2 Click . . . . **Fo̲rmat, Ce̲lls...**

OR

  a Right-click . . . . *any selected cell*

  b Click . . . . **Format Cells...**

FROM PATTERNS

To select a color for cells:

  • Click desired color on . . . . *C̲olor palette*

To select a pattern for cells:

  a Select a pattern in . . . . **Pa̲ttern:**

  b Select a color for pattern in . . . . . **Pa̲ttern:**

3 Click . . . . OK

Format Number, Date, or Time

1 Select . . . . ***cell(s)***

2 Click . . . . **Fo̲rmat, Ce̲lls...**

OR

  a Right-click . . . . ***any selected cell***

  b Click . . . . **Format Cells...**

> *FROM NUMBER*

3 Select a category in . . . . **Ca̲tegory:** *list*
Categories include: General, Number, Currency, Accounting,
Date, Time, Percentage, Fraction, Scientific, Text, Special, Custom

4 Select option(s) for selected category.

5 Click . . . . ▢ OK ▢

Apply Common Number Formats ▶
Using Toolbar

• Select . . . . ***cell(s)***

  – FROM FORMATTING TOOLBAR –

To apply currency style:

  • Click . . . . ***Currency Style button*** ▢ $ ▢

To apply percent style:

  • Click . . . . ***Percent Style button*** ▢ % ▢

To apply the comma style:

  • Click . . . . ***Comma Style button*** ▢ , ▢

To increase or decrease decimal places:

  • Click . . . . ***Increase Decimal button*** ▢ .00 ▢

  OR

  Click . . . . ***Decrease Decimal button*** ▢ .00 ▢

Create or Delete a Custom Number Format

1 Click .... F**o**rmat, C**e**lls...

⌐———————— *FROM NUMBER* ————————⌐

To create a custom number format:

a Select Custom in .... **C**ategory: *list*

b Type or edit number codes in .... **T**ype: [   ]

NOTE: Editing codes in T̲ype box will not delete the format from the T̲ype list. To look up valid codes, search Excel's Help Topics under the Index tab for **number formats, custom number formats***.*

To delete a custom number format:

a Select Custom in .... **C**ategory: *list*

b Select code to delete in .... **T**ype: *list*

c Click .... [Delete]

2 Click .... [OK]

NOTE: Excel saves custom number formats when you save the workbook.

Hide Data in Cells

Creates a custom format that hides data in cells. The hidden data can be viewed by selecting the cell and reading the data in the formula bar.

1 Select .... *cell(s)*

2 Click .... F**o**rmat, C**e**lls...

⌐———————— *FROM NUMBER* ————————⌐

3 Select Custom in .... **C**ategory: *list*

4 Type ;;; (three semicolons) in .... **T**ype: [   ]

NOTE: Deleting codes in T̲ype box will not delete the format from the T̲ype list.

5 Click .... [OK]

Clear All Formats Applied to Cells

1 Select . . . . *cell(s)*

2 Click . . . . <u>E</u>dit, Cle<u>a</u>r ▸, <u>F</u>ormats

Copy Formats ▸ Using Toolbar

• Select . . . . *cell(s) containing formats to copy*

To copy formats <u>once</u>:

a Click . . . . *Format Painter button* 🖌️
on Standard toolbar.
Pointer changes to a ⊕🖌️

b Select . . . . *cell* or *range of cells*
where you want to apply the formats.

To copy formats <u>multiple times</u>:

a Double-click . . . . *Format Painter button* 🖌️
on Standard toolbar.
Pointer changes to a ⊕🖌️

b Select . . . . *destination cell(s)*

c Repeat step **b**, as desired.

d Click . . . . *Format Painter button* 🖌️
to end copying.

Create a Style ▶ by Example

1 Select . . . . *cell containing desired formats*

2 Click . . . . **F̲ormat, S̲tyle...**

3 Type a name for style in . . . . . . **S̲tyle Name:** [▼]
Excel displays the style's formats in Style Includes box.

To exclude formats of selected cell from style:

- Deselect . . . . **Style Includes (By Example) options:**
  N̲umber, F̲ont, Al̲ignment, B̲order, P̲atterns, Pr̲otection

4 Click . . . . [OK   ]

Create a Style ▶ by Defining It

1 Click . . . . **F̲ormat, S̲tyle...**

2 Type a name for style in . . . . . . **S̲tyle Name:** [▼]

To exclude formats of selected cell from style:

- Deselect . . . . **Style Includes options:**
  N̲umber, F̲ont, Al̲ignment, B̲order, P̲atterns, Pr̲otection

3 Click . . . . [Modify...]

4 Click . . . . *tab of format category to include*
Tab options include: Number, Alignment, Font, Border,
Patterns, Protection

5 Select options for selected tab.

6 Repeat steps 4 and 5 for each format category to include.

7 Click . . . . [OK   ]

To define and apply style:

- Click . . . . [OK   ]

To define style without applying it:

a Click . . . . [Add   ]

b Click . . . . [Close   ]

Redefine a Style ▶ by Example

1 Select . . . . *cell*
containing formats to assign to style.

2 Click . . . . **F̲ormat, S̲tyle...**

3 T̲ype (do not select) name of
style to redefine in . . . . **S̲tyle Name:** [_____ ▾]

4 Click . . . . [A̲dd...]

If Redefine prompt appears,

● Click . . . . [Y̲es]

5 Click . . . . [OK]

Redefine a Style ▶ by Defining It

1 Click . . . . **F̲ormat, S̲tyle...**

2 Select name of style
to redefine in . . . . **S̲tyle Name:** [_____ ▾]

To exclude format categories from style:

● Deselect . . . . *Style Includes options:*
N̲umber, F̲ont, A̲lignment, B̲order, P̲atterns, P̲rotection

To change formats:

a Click . . . . [M̲odify...]

b Click . . . . *tab of format category to change*
Tab options include: Number, Alignment, Font, Border,
Patterns, Protection

c Select options for selected tab.

d Repeat steps **b** and **c** for each format category to change.

e Click . . . . [OK]

3 Click . . . . [OK]

Apply a Style

NOTE: *If you use styles often, consider adding the Style box to the Formatting toolbar. (See* **Add or Remove Toolbar Buttons** *on page 25.) You can then select or define styles quickly without opening menus.*

1 Select . . . . *cell(s) to which to apply style*

2 Click . . . . **F**ormat, **S**tyle...

3 Select style name in . . . . **S**tyle Name: [▼]

4 Click . . . . [OK]

Copy Styles from Another Workbook

1 Open . . . . *source and destination workbooks*

2 Select . . . . *destination workbook*

3 Click . . . . **F**ormat, **S**tyle...

4 Click . . . . [**M**erge...]

5 Select name of source workbook in . . . **M**erge Styles From: *list*

6 Click . . . . [OK]

If merge styles message appears,

- Click . . . . [**Y**es]
  to replace styles in destination workbook that have the same name.

  OR

  Click . . . . [**N**o]
  to retain styles that have the same names in destination workbook.

7 Click . . . . [OK]

Delete a Style

1 Click .... **Fo̱rmat, S̱tyle...**

2 Select name of style to delete in.. **S̱tyle Name:** [⬚ |▼]

> *NOTE: Normal style cannot be deleted.*

3 Click .... [De̱lete]

4 Click .... [OK]

AutoFormat Worksheet Data

Applies built-in formats to data in a range, list, or pivot table.

1 Select .... *any cell in data block to format*

> *NOTE: The data block can be a list or a pivot table.*

2 Click .... **Fo̱rmat, A̱utoFormat...**

3 Select desired format in .... **Ṯable Format:** *list*

To exclude parts of format:

a Click .... [O̱ptions >>]

b Deselect .... ***Formats to Apply options:***
Number, Ḇorder, F̱ont, P̱atterns, A̱lignment, W̱idth/Height

4 Click .... [OK]

Clear an AutoFormat

1 Select .... *any cell in formatted range*

2 Click .... **Fo̱rmat, A̱utoFormat...**

3 Select None in .... **Ṯable Format:** *list*

4 Click .... [OK]

Open the Page Setup Dialog Box

Sets page, margins, headers, footers, and sheet options for printing.

1 Select .... ***sheet(s) to print***
*NOTE: When printing a group of sheets of different types,
the settings you select will affect only the active sheet and
all sheets of the same type. Therefore, you should repeat
these steps for each sheet type when printing a group.*

OR

Select .... ***cells to print***

To open Page Setup from workbook:

• Click .... **File, Page Setup...**

To open Page Setup from Print Preview:

a Click .... ***Print Preview button*** [image]
on Standard toolbar.

b Click .... | Setup... |

2 Select .... ***Page Setup options:***

Refer to the following topics:
Set Page Options *(page 162) to set print options for page orientation,
scaling of data on page, paper size, print quality, first page number.*
Set Print Margins *(page 163) to set print options for page margins,
header and footer margins, and center data on page.*
Set Header and Footer Options *(page 164) to set up repeating text
or codes (such as a page number) to print on the top and bottom
of each page.*
Set Print Options for Sheet *(page 165) to set print options for print area,
print titles, gridlines, notes, row and column headings, black and white
printing, page order.*
Set Print Options for Chart *(page 167) to set chart size and print quality.*

162

Set Page Options

Sets page orientation, scaling of data on page, paper size, print quality, first page number.

1 Open (page 161) . . . . ***Page Setup dialog box***

─────────────┌──────────────────────┐─────────────
             │   *FROM PAGE*   │
─────────────┘   └─────────────

NOTE: Available options will depend on the currently selected printer.

To set page <u>orientation</u>:

• Select . . . . ◯ **Por<u>t</u>rait** or ◯ **<u>L</u>andscape**

To <u>scale</u> data on printed sheet:

a Select . . . . ◯ **<u>A</u>djust to:**

b Type or select percentage (10-400)
to reduce or enlarge data in . . . . [|⭥] **% normal size**

To <u>fit sheet(s)</u> on a specific number of pages:

NOTE: Excel ignores manual page breaks when this setting is selected. Not available for chart sheets.

a Select . . . . ◯ **<u>F</u>it to:**

b Type or select number
of pages in . . . . . [|⭥] **page(s) wide by** [|⭥] **tall**

To set <u>paper size</u>:

• Select paper size in . . . . **Paper Si<u>z</u>e:** [|▼]

To set <u>print quality</u>:

• Select print resolution in . . . **Print <u>Q</u>uality:** [|▼]

To specify <u>first page number</u>:

• Type Auto or number in . . . **Fi<u>r</u>st Page Number:** [ ]

2 Click . . . . **Page Setup tab** or **command button**

Page Setup tabs: *Margins, Header/Footer, Sheet/Chart*
Command buttons: *OK, Cancel, <u>P</u>rint..., Print Preview, <u>O</u>ptions...*

Set Print Margins

Sets page margins, header and footer margins, and centers data on page.

1 Open (page 161) . . . . *Page Setup dialog box*

─────────┌────── *FROM MARGINS* ──────┐─────────

To set <u>page</u> margins:

- Type or select number
  for margins in . . . . . . **<u>T</u>op, <u>B</u>ottom, <u>L</u>eft, <u>R</u>ight**   [____]⬍

To set <u>header and footer</u> margins:

NOTE: *To prevent data from overlapping, these settings should be less than the top and bottom margin settings.*

- Type or select number for margin in . . . **He<u>a</u>der:**   [____]⬍

AND/OR

- Type or select number for margin in . . . **<u>F</u>ooter:**   [____]⬍

To set page <u>alignment</u>:

- Select . . . . ☐ **Hori<u>z</u>ontally** and/or ☐ **<u>V</u>ertically**
  NOTE: *For chart sheets, you must first select Custom from the Chart tab, page 167.*

2 Click . . . . *Page Setup tab* or *command button*
Page Setup tabs: *Page, Header/Footer, Sheet/Chart*
Command buttons: *OK, Cancel, <u>P</u>rint..., Print Previe<u>w</u>, <u>O</u>ptions...*

Set Header and Footer Options

Adds repeating text or special codes to the top or bottom of each page.

1 Open (page 161) . . . . ***Page Setup dialog box***

> FROM *HEADER/FOOTER*

To select a <u>built-in header</u>:

- Select a header in . . . . **He<u>a</u>der:** [▼]

To select a <u>built-in footer</u>:

- Select a footer in . . . . **<u>F</u>ooter:** [▼]

To <u>customize header</u>:

a Select header to customize in . . . . **He<u>a</u>der:** [▼]

b Click . . . . [<u>C</u>ustom Header...]

then continue to step **c** below.

OR

To <u>customize footer</u>:

a Select footer to customize in . . . . **<u>F</u>ooter:** [▼]

b Click . . . . [Cu<u>s</u>tom Footer...]

then continue to step **c** below.

c Click in . . . . **Section to change**
   Sections include: <u>L</u>eft Section, <u>C</u>enter Section, <u>R</u>ight Section

d Type or edit . . . . ***text***

To format header or footer text:

1. Select . . . . ***text***
2. Click . . . . ***Font button*** [A]
3. Select . . . . ***Font options***
4. Click . . . . [OK]

Continued ...

Set Header and Footer Options (continued)

To insert header/footer code at insertion point:

- Click .... *desired code button:*

🔢	**Page Number**	*inserts page number code*
📑	**Total Pages**	*inserts total pages code*
📅	**Date**	*inserts current date code*
🕗	**Time**	*inserts current time code*
📄	**Filename**	*inserts filename code*
🖵	**Sheet Name**	*inserts active sheet name code*

e Repeat steps **c** and **d** for each section to change.

f Click .... | OK |

2 Click .... *Page Setup tab* or *command button*
  Page Setup tabs: *Page, Margins, Sheet/Chart*
  Command buttons: *OK, Cancel, Print..., Print Preview, Options...*

Set Print Options for Sheet

Sets print options for area, titles, gridlines, notes, row and column headings, black and white printing, and page order.

1 Open (page 161) .... *Page Setup dialog box*
  NOTE: You can not open the Page Setup dialog box from Print Preview to specify a print area or set repeating print titles.

```
             FROM SHEET
```

To define a print area:

- Select (in worksheet) or
  type reference(s) to print in ...... **Print Area:** [   ]
  NOTE: Separate each range or range name with a comma.
  To remove a print area, delete the reference.

To set rows as repeating print titles:

- Select rows (in worksheet) or type reference
  to rows in .... **Rows to Repeat at Top:** [   ]
  NOTE: Rows must be adjacent. To remove print titles,
  delete the reference.

Continued ...

Set Print Options for Sheet (continued)

To set columns as repeating <u>print titles</u>:

- Select columns (in worksheet)
  or type reference
  to columns in .... **Columns to Repeat at Left:** [ ]

  NOTE: Columns must be adjacent. To remove print titles, delete the reference.

To set printing of <u>gridlines</u>:

- Select or deselect .... ☐ **<u>G</u>ridlines**

To print <u>notes</u>:

a Select .... ☐ **<u>N</u>otes**

b Deselect .... ☐ **Row and Co<u>l</u>umn Headings**

To print <u>notes</u> (with references):

a Select .... ☐ **<u>N</u>otes**

b Select .... ☐ **Row and Co<u>l</u>umn Headings**

To set printing to <u>draft quality</u>:

- Select .... ☐ **Draft <u>Q</u>uality**

To set printing to <u>black and white</u>:

- Select .... ☐ **<u>B</u>lack and White**

To print <u>row and column headings</u>:

- Select .... ☐ **Row and Co<u>l</u>umn Headings**

To set <u>page order</u>:

- Select .... ○ **<u>D</u>own, then Across**

  OR

  Select .... ○ **Acro<u>s</u>s, then Down**

2 Click .... ***Page Setup tab*** or ***command button***

Page Setup tabs: *Page, Margins, Header/Footer*
Command buttons: *OK, Cancel, <u>P</u>rint..., Print Previe<u>w</u>, <u>O</u>ptions...*

Set Print Options for Chart

Sets printed chart size and print quality.

1 Enable (page 196) . . . . *chart editing*

2 Open (page 161) . . . . *Page Setup dialog box*

FROM CHART

NOTE: Available options will depend on the currently selected printer.

To set printed chart <u>size</u>:

- Select . . . . ○ **Use Full Page**

  or . . . . ○ Scale to <u>F</u>it Page

  or . . . . ○ **<u>C</u>ustom**

  NOTE: With Custom selected you can align the chart, page 163.

To set print <u>quality</u> of chart

- Select . . . . □ **Draft <u>Q</u>uality**

To print chart in <u>black and white</u>:

- Select . . . . □ **Print in <u>B</u>lack and White**

3 Click . . . . *Page Setup tab* or *command button*

Page Setup tabs: *Page, Margins, Header/Footer*
Command buttons: *OK, Cancel, <u>P</u>rint..., Print Previe<u>w</u>, <u>O</u>ptions...*

Set Print Area Quickly

1 Select . . . . *cell range(s) to print*

2 Click . . . . **<u>F</u>ile, Prin<u>t</u> Area ▸, <u>S</u>et Print Area**

Clear Print Area Quickly

- Click . . . . **<u>F</u>ile, Prin<u>t</u> Area ▸, <u>C</u>lear Print Area**

Print Preview

1 Before previewing, set page options (page 162) and select sheet(s) to print.

2 Click .... ***Print Preview button*** 🔲
on Standard toolbar.

NOTE: To preview how selected cells will print, you must open the Preview window from the Print dialog box (File, Print).

To view next/previous page:

• Click .... | Next | or | Previous |

To magnify portion of page:

• Click .... ***area of page to magnify***

To return to full page view:

• Click .... ***any area of page***

To change page settings:

a Click .... | Setup... |

b Select page setup options (page 161).

To change margin and columns:

a Click .... | Margins |

b Drag .... ***margin handle*** or ***column handle***
to desired position.

NOTE: Status bar displays size as you drag handle.

To print page:

a Click .... | Print... |

b Select print options (page 171).

To exit Print Preview:

• Click .... | Close |

Manual Page Breaks

NOTE: *After you insert or remove a manual page break, Excel adjusts the automatic page breaks that follow it. To display automatic page breaks see* **Show Automatic Page Breaks,** *below.*

Insert Horizontal Page Break
1 Select . . . . *row where new page will start*
2 Click . . . . <u>I</u>nsert, Page <u>B</u>reak

Insert Vertical Page Break
1 Select . . . . *column where new page will start*
2 Click . . . . <u>I</u>nsert, Page <u>B</u>reak

Insert Horizontal and Vertical Page Breaks
1 Select . . . . *cell where new pages will start*
2 Click . . . . <u>I</u>nsert, Page <u>B</u>reak

Remove Horizontal Page Break
1 Select . . . . *cell immediately below page break*
2 Click . . . . <u>I</u>nsert, Remove Page <u>B</u>reak

Remove Vertical Page Break
1 Select . . . . . . *cell immediately to the right of page break*
2 Click . . . . <u>I</u>nsert, Remove Page <u>B</u>reak

Remove All Manual Page Breaks
1 Click . . . . *Select All button* ☐
2 Click . . . . <u>I</u>nsert, Remove Page <u>B</u>reak

Show Automatic Page Breaks

1 Click . . . . <u>T</u>ools, <u>O</u>ptions...

FROM VIEW

2 Select . . . . ☐ A<u>u</u>tomatic Page Breaks
3 Click . . . . [OK]

Select Printer

1 Click . . . .**File, Print...**

2 Select printer in . . . . **Name:** | ⬛ |

To change printer settings:

a Click . . . . [Properties...]

b Select . . . . *printer settings*
NOTE: Printer settings may include Paper (paper size, layout, orientation, source, copies), Graphics (resolution, halftoning, scaling), Device Options (printer features), PostScript.

c Click . . . . [OK]

3 Click . . . . [OK]
to select printer and print.

OR

Click . . . . [Cancel]
to select printer and close dialog box.

Print Sheets ► Using Toolbar

1 Select . . . . *sheet to print*

OR

Select . . . . *any sheet in group to print*
NOTE: If you defined a print area, Excel will print only the print area(s) you defined. (See **Clear Print Area Quickly***, page 167.)*

2 Click . . . . *Print button* 🖨
on Standard toolbar.

Print

Prints workbook data using current page settings (page 161).

1 Select . . . . *range(s) in worksheet(s) to print*
NOTE: *Non-adjacent ranges print on separate pages.*
This procedure overrides defined print areas.

OR

Select . . . . . *sheet to print* or *any sheet in group to print*
NOTE: *Excel will only print a print area (pages 165 and 167)*
if you defined one.

2 Click . . . . **File, Print...**
3 Select . . . . **Print What option:**

- Click . . . . ◯ **Selection**
- Click . . . . ◯ **Selected Sheet(s)**
- Click . . . . ◯ **Entire Workbook**

NOTE: *When printing selected sheets or the entire workbook,*
Excel will print only sheets containing data.

To set number of copies:

a Type or select number in . . . **Number of copies:** [ ] ⬍

b Select or deselect . . . . ☐ **Collate**
NOTE: *Select Collate to print multiple copies as complete sets.*

To set page range to print:

- Select . . . . ◯ **All**

OR

a Select . . . . ◯ **Pages**
b Type or select first page number in . . . . . **from:** [ ] ⬍
c Type or select last page number in . . . . **to:** [ ] ⬍

4 Click . . . . [OK]

Create or Edit a Report

NOTE: *To create a report you must first install Report Manager.*
See Install or Remove an Add-In, page 179.

1 Click .... **View, Report Manager...**

2 a Click .... | Add... |
to create a report.

  b Type a name for report in ..... **Report Name:** | |

OR

  a Select name of report to edit in .... **Reports:** *list*

  b Click .... | Edit... |

To create sections for the report:

  a Select sheet for section in .... **Sheet:** | ▼ |

  b If desired, select view and/or scenario for selected sheet.

  c Click .... | Add |

  d Repeat steps **a-c** for each section to create.

To change print order of a report section:

  a Select section to move in .. **Sections in this Report:** *list*

  b Click .... | Move Up | or | Move Down |

To delete a report section:

  a Select section to delete in .. **Sections in this Report:** *list*

  b Click .... | Delete |

To number report pages consecutively:

  • Select .... ☐ Use **C**ontinuous Page Numbers

3 Click .... | OK |

4 Click .... | Print... |

OR

Click .... | Close |

Print Report

1 Click .... **V**iew, **R**eport Manager...

2 Select name of report to print in .... **Reports:** *list*

3 Click .... Print...

4 Type number of copies to print in .... **C**opies:

5 Click .... OK

Name a View of a Worksheet

NOTE: *Excel saves named views with the worksheet. Views can be printed, displayed, or added to a report.*

1 If desired, define (page 165 and 167) .... *print area for view*

2 Set .... *display options for view*
NOTE: *Excel stores the following settings: window size, window position, active cell, frozen panes, frozen titles, outlining, zoom percentage, print settings, hidden columns and rows, and many view options.*

3 Click .... **V**iew, **V**iew Manager...
NOTE: *If View Manager does not appear on the View menu, see Install or Remove an Add-In, page 179.*

4 Click .... Add...

5 Type name for view in .... **N**ame:

To exclude current print settings from view:

● Deselect .... ☑ **P**rint Settings

To exclude hidden columns and rows from view:

● Deselect .... ☑ Hidden **R**ows & Columns

6 Click .... OK

Display a View of a Worksheet

1 Select . . . . . *worksheet containing named view to display*

2 Click . . . . **View, View Manager...**

3 Select name of view to display in . . . . **Views:** *list*

4 Click . . . . | Show |

Delete a View of a Worksheet

1 Select . . . . . . *worksheet containing named view to delete*

2 Click . . . . **View, View Manager...**

3 Select name of view to delete in . . . . **Views:** *list*

4 Click . . . . | Delete |

5 Click . . . . | OK |
to confirm deletion.

6 Click . . . . | Close |

Print a View of a Worksheet

1 Select . . . . *worksheet containing named view to print*

2 Click . . . . **View, View Manager...**

3 Select name of view to print in . . . . **Views:** *list*

4 Click . . . . | Show |

5 Click . . . . *Print button* 🖨
on Standard toolbar.

Split Worksheet into Panes ▶
Using Split Boxes

Provides simultaneous scrolling of up to four panes. You can freeze panes (page 176) to prevent the top and/or left panes from scrolling.

*NOTE: If the scroll bars are not displayed, see **Set View Options**, page 179.*

1 Point to .... *horizontal split box* ▭ or *vertical split box* []
on scroll bar.

Pointer becomes a ╪ or ╫

2 Drag .... ╪ or ╫ *along scroll bar*
until split bar is in desired position.

Split Worksheet into Panes ▶
Using Menu

Provides simultaneous scrolling of up to four panes. You can freeze panes (page 176) to prevent the top and/or left panes from scrolling.

1 Select .... *row*
below which horizontal split will occur.

or .... *column*
to right of which vertical split will occur.

or .... *cell below and to the right*
of which horizontal and vertical split will occur.

2 Click .... Window, Split

Remove Split Bars

• Double-click .... *any part of split bar*

OR

• Click .... Window, Remove Split

Adjust Worksheet Panes

1 Point to . . . . *horizontal or vertical split bar*
Pointer becomes a ╪ or ╫
2 Drag . . . . *split bar outline*
to desired position.

Move Between Worksheet Panes

• Click . . . . *desired pane*
OR
• Press . . . . `F6`
until active cell is in desired pane.

Freeze Panes on a Split Worksheet

Locks top and/or left pane when scrolling.
• Click . . . . **W**indow, **F**reeze Panes

Unfreeze Panes

• Click . . . . **W**indow, Unf**r**eeze Panes

Freeze Titles

Locks display of title row and/or title column on the screen. This procedure is for a worksheet that has not been split into panes.

1 Select . . . . ***row***
below horizontal titles to freeze.

or . . . . ***column***
to right of vertical titles to freeze.

or . . . . ***cell below and to the right***
of horizontal and vertical titles to freeze.

2 Click . . . . <u>W</u>indow, <u>F</u>reeze Panes

Unfreeze Titles

• Click . . . . <u>W</u>indow, Un<u>f</u>reeze Panes

Display a Sheet Full Screen

Maximizes the sheet window and removes the status bar as well as any toolbars.

1 Select . . . . ***sheet to view full screen***

2 Click . . . . <u>V</u>iew, F<u>u</u>ll Screen
Excel displays sheet full screen and the Full Screen button on a toolbar.

End Full Screen View

• Click . . . . **Full Screen button**

OR

• Click . . . . <u>V</u>iew, ✓ F<u>u</u>ll Screen

Zoom ▸ Using Toolbar

Changes the scale of worksheet(s), chart sheet(s), or selected range of cells.

Set Magnification for Worksheets or Chart Sheets

NOTE: *To set a zoom percentage for chart sheets, you must first deselect the Sized with Window option from the View menu.*

1 Select . . . . ***sheet(s) to scale***

2 Enter a number (10-400), or
   select a zoom percentage in . . . . ***Zoom Control*** [￮|▼]
   on Standard toolbar.

Fit Range of Cells to Current Window Size

1 Select . . . . ***range of cells to magnify***

2 Select **Selection** in . . . . ***Zoom Control*** [￮|▼]
   on Standard toolbar.

Zoom ▸ Using Menu

Changes the scale of worksheet(s), chart sheet(s), or selected cells.

Set Magnification for Worksheets or Chart Sheets

NOTE: *To set a zoom percentage for chart sheets, you must first deselect the Sized with Window option from the View menu.*

1 Select . . . . ***sheet(s) to scale***

2 Click . . . . ***View, Zoom...***

3 Select . . . . ***Magnification option:***
   200%, 100%, 75%, 50%, 25%

   OR

   a Select . . . . ◯ **Custom**

   b Type zoom percentage (10-400) in . . . . [＿＿＿] %

4 Click . . . . [OK]

Fit Selected Range to Current Window Size

1 Click . . . . ***View, Zoom...***

2 Select . . . . ◯ **Fit Selection**

3 Click . . . . [OK]

Set View Options

Sets display of many workspace and window elements.

1 Click .... **Tools,** **Options...**

```
                  ┌─────── FROM VIEW ───────┐
```

To set **general** view options:

● Select or deselect .... **Show options:**
  Formula Bar, Status Bar, Note Indicator, Info Window
  NOTE: These selections are not saved with workbook.

To set view of **graphic objects**:

● Select .... **Objects options:**
  Show All – select to show all graphic objects.
  Show Placeholders – select to show gray rectangles where pictures
  and embedded charts will appear when printed.
  Hide All – select to hide graphic objects. Hidden objects will not print.

To set view of **window** options:

● Select or deselect .... **Window options:**
  Automatic Page Breaks, Formulas, Gridlines, Gridlines Color,
  Row & Column Headers, Outline Symbols, Zero Values,
  Horizontal Scroll Bar, Vertical Scroll Bar, Sheet Tabs

2 Click .... [OK]

Install or Remove an Add-In

Add-ins are programs or functions you can add to Excel menus.
They include AccessLinks Add-In, Analysis ToolPak, Analysis ToolPak-VBA,
AutoSave, MS Query Add-In, ODBC Add-In, Report Manager, Solver Add-In,
Template Utilities, Template Wizard with Data Tracking, Update Add-in Links,
View Manager.

1 Click .... **Tools,** **Add-Ins...**

2 Select or deselect add-ins in .... **Add-Ins Available:** *list*
  NOTE: You can click the Browse button
  to locate add-ins in other directories.

3 Click .... [OK]

Protect a Workbook

Prevents user from changing the way a workbook is arranged or displayed.

1 Select or open . . . . ***workbook to protect***

2 Click . . . . **T**ools, **P**rotection ▸, Protect **W**orkbook...

To set password protection:

• Type password in . . . . . . **P**assword (optional): [   ]

To protect workbook structure:

Prevents sheets from being inserted, deleted, renamed, moved, hidden, or unhidden.

• Select . . . . ☐ **S**tructure

To protect workbook windows:

Prevents windows from being closed, sized, moved, hidden, or unhidden.

• Select . . . . ☐ **W**indows

3 Click . . . . [OK]

If a password was typed,

a Retype password in . . . . [   ]

b Click . . . . [OK]

Unprotect a Workbook

1 Select or open . . . . ***workbook to unprotect***

2 Click . . **T**ools, **P**rotection ▸, Unprotect **W**orkbook...

If workbook is password protected,

a Type password in . . . . **P**assword: [   ]

b Click . . . . [OK]

Protect a Sheet

Prevents changes to locked cells, graphic objects, embedded charts in a worksheet or chart items in a chart sheet. By default, all cells and objects in a worksheet are locked (page 182).

1 Select . . . . *sheet to protect*

2 Click . . . . **Tools, Protection** ►, **Protect Sheet...**

To password protect sheet:

- Type password in . . . . . . **Password (optional):** [   ]

To protect cell contents and chart items:

- Select . . . . ☐ **Contents**

To protect graphic objects:

- Select . . . . ☐ **Objects**

To protect scenarios:

- Select . . . . ☐ **Scenarios**

3 Click . . . . [OK]

If a password was typed,

a Retype password in . . . . [   ]

b Click . . . . [OK]

Unprotect a Sheet

1 Select . . . . *sheet to unprotect*

2 Click . . . . . . **Tools, Protection** ►, **Unprotect Sheet...**

If sheet is password protected,

a Type password in . . . . **Password:** [   ]

b Click . . . . [OK]

Lock Cells or Graphic Objects

Unlocks or locks specific cells or graphic objects. By default, all cells and objects in a worksheet are locked. Locking takes effect when a sheet is protected (page 181).

1 If necessary, unprotect (page 181) . . . . **sheet**

2 Select . . . . **cell(s)** or **graphic object(s)**
to unlock or lock.

3 a Click . . . . **Format**

b Click . . . **Cells...** or **Object...** or **Selected Object...**
NOTE: *You can press Ctrl+1 to access format options quickly.*

FROM PROTECTION

4 Select or deselect . . . . □ **Locked**

To lock/unlock text in a text box:

• Select or deselect . . . . □ **Lock Text**

5 Click . . . . | OK |

6 Repeat steps 2-5 for each cell or object to lock or unlock.

7 Protect (page 181) . . . . **sheet**
to enable locking.

Hide or Unhide Formulas

Hidden formulas will not appear on the formula bar. When you hide a formula, the setting takes effect when a sheet is protected (page 181).

1 If necessary, unprotect (page 181) . . . . **sheet**

2 Select . . . . **cells containing formulas to hide**

3 Click . . . . **Format, Cells...**

FROM PROTECTION

4 Select or deselect . . . . □ **Hidden**

5 Click . . . . | OK |

6 Protect (page 181) . . . . **worksheet contents**
to enable hidden formulas.

Graphic Objects

Examples of graphic objects include lines, arcs, arrows, rectangles, ellipses, embedded charts, text boxes, buttons and imported graphics. These objects can be inserted into a worksheet or chart sheet.

Select Graphic Objects

Select One Graphic Object

- Click . . . . *object*
  Excel marks object with a selection outline and handles.

  OR

  If a macro has been assigned to the graphic object,

  a Click . . . . *Drawing button*
  on Standard toolbar to show Drawing toolbar.

  b Click . . . . *Drawing Selection button*

  c Click . . . . *any part of object*
  Excel marks object with a selection outline and handles.

  NOTE: *When you have finished editing the object, click the Drawing Selection button again to allow macros to run.*

Select Multiple Graphic Objects

- Press <u>Shift</u> and click . . . . *each object*
  Excel marks object(s) with a selection outline and handles.

  OR

  If a macro has been assigned to any of the graphic objects,

  a Click . . . . *Drawing button*
  on Standard toolbar to show Drawing toolbar.

  b Click . . . . *Drawing Selection button*

  c Drag . . . . *selection outline around objects*
  Excel marks object(s) with a selection outline and handles.

  To add or remove objects:

  - Press <u>Shift</u> and click . . . . *each object*

  NOTE: *When you have finished editing the objects, click the Drawing Selection button again to allow macros to run.*

Create a Text Box

1 Click . . . . *Drawing button* 🖱️
on Standard toolbar to show Drawing toolbar.

2 Click . . . . *Text Box button* 📓
on Drawing toolbar.
Pointer becomes a +

3 Position . . . . +
where corner of box will be.

To create a box without constraints:

- Drag . . . . *box outline*
  until desired size is obtained.

To create a square box:

- Press <u>Shift</u> and drag . . . . *box outline*
  until desired size is obtained.

To create a box and align it to gridlines:

- Press <u>Alt</u> and drag . . . . *box outline*
  until desired size is obtained.

4 Type . . . . *text as desired*

5 Click . . . . *outside text box*
to return to normal operations.

Edit Text in a Text Box

1 Select . . . . *text box*

To replace existing text with new text:

- Type . . . . *new text*

To edit existing text:

a Click . . . . *desired character position*

b Insert and delete . . . . *characters as desired*

2 Click . . . . *outside text box*
to return to normal operations.

Link Text Box Text to Contents of a Cell

1 Select . . . . *text box*

2 Click in . . . . *formula bar*

3 Type . . . . ▣
then select (in worksheet)
or type . . . . *reference to cell containing text*
EXAMPLE: =A4

4 Enter . . . . ↵

Change Font in Text Box

1 Select . . . . *text box*

2 Drag . . . . *highlight over text to format*
NOTE: *If text is linked to a worksheet cell, you cannot format partial text.*

3 Click . . . . F̱ormat
then click . . . . Obj̱ect... or S̱elected Object...
NOTE: *You can also click buttons on the Formatting toolbar to format the text quickly.*

4 Select . . . . *Font options*
(See **Change Font ▸ Using Menu**, *page 150.*)

5 Click . . . . | OK |

Change Text Alignment in Text Box

1 Select . . . . *text box*
NOTE: *Do not click text in text box.*

2 Click . . . . **F̲ormat**
then click . . . . **Obj̲ect...** or **S̲elected Object...**
NOTE: *You can also click buttons on toolbar to align text quickly.*

FROM *ALIGNMENT*

To align text horizontally:

- Select . . . . *Horizontal option:*
  L̲eft, C̲enter, R̲ight, J̲ustify

To align text vertically:

- Select . . . . *Vertical option:*
  T̲op, C̲enter, B̲ottom, J̲ustify

To change orientation of text:

- Select . . . . *Orientation option*

To automatically size text box to fit text:

- Select . . . . ☐ **A̲utomatic Size**

3 Click . . . . [OK]

Draw Graphic Objects

Draws objects such as rectangles and ellipses.

1 Click . . . . *Drawing button* 🖊
on Standard toolbar to show Drawing toolbar.
NOTE: *You can rest pointer on a button in the Drawing toolbar
to show its name.*

2 Click . . . . *desired drawing tool*
on Drawing toolbar.
Pointer becomes a ╋ *and the status bar displays instructions.*

3 Point to . . . . . *an area where a corner of object will begin*

4 Drag . . . . *object's outline*
until desired size and shape is obtained.

Change Border or Fill of Graphic Objects

1 Select . . . . *graphic object(s)*

2 Click . . . . **F̲ormat**
then click . . . . **Obj̲ect...** or **S̲elected Object...**
NOTE: You can also double-click object to access format options.

> FROM PATTERNS

To change <u>line or border</u> style:

- Select . . . . *Line or Border options:*
  A̲utomatic – *to return object to default setting.*
  N̲one – *to make selection invisible.*
  Shad̲ow – *to add shadow to rectangles, ellipses, charts or text boxes.*
  R̲ound Corners – *to round corners of rectangles, charts and text boxes.*
  Custom – *to allow for custom formatting.*

  If Custom,

  a Select line or border
  style in . . . . **St̲yle:** [▼]

  b Select line or border
  color in . . . . **C̲olor:** [▼]

  c Select line or border
  thickness in . . . . **W̲eight:** [▼]

To change or add an <u>arrow</u> style to a line:

- Select . . . . *Arrowhead options:*
  Style, Wi̲dth, L̲ength
  NOTE: To add an arrow to a line, you must first select an arrow style before selecting a width or length.

To <u>fill</u> object with color or pattern:

- Select . . . . *Fill options:*
  A̲utomatic – *to return object to default setting.*
  Non̲e – *to remove fill.*
  Color palette – to add fills to rectangles, ellipses, charts or text boxes.
  P̲attern – *to add a pattern to selection. To color the pattern, select
  P̲attern again.*

3 Click . . . . [OK]

Move Graphic Objects

1 Select . . . . *graphic object(s)* or *chart item*

2 Point to . . . . *border of any selected object*
Pointer becomes a ⬉

3 Drag . . . . *border outline*
to desired position.

OR

Press <u>Alt</u> and drag . . . . *border outline*
to align object to gridlines.

Copy Graphic Objects

1 Select . . . . *graphic object(s)* or *chart item*

2 Point to . . . . *border of any selected object*
Pointer becomes a ⬉

3 Press <u>Ctrl</u> and drag . . . . *border outline*
to desired position.

OR

Press <u>Ctrl+Alt</u> and drag . . . . *border outline*
to align object to gridlines.

Size Graphic Objects

1 Select . . . . *graphic object(s)* or *chart item*

2 Point to . . . . *selection handle*
on side of border to size.
Pointer becomes a ⬂ ↔ ⬈ ↕

To size object without constraints:

- Drag . . . . *border outline*
  until desired size is obtained.

To size object and align to gridlines:

- Press <u>Alt</u> and drag . . . . *border outline*
  until desired size is obtained.

Delete Graphic Objects

1 Select . . . . *graphic object(s)* or *chart item*

2 Press . . . . `Del`

Overlap Graphic Objects

1 Select . . . . *graphic object(s)* or *chart item*

2 Click . . . . *Drawing button*
on Standard toolbar to show Drawing toolbar.

3 Click . . . . *Bring To Front button*

OR

Click . . . . *Send To Back button*

Group Graphic Objects

1 Click . . . . *Drawing button*
on Standard toolbar to show Drawing toolbar.

2 Select . . . . *graphic objects to group*

3 Click . . . . *Group Objects button*

Ungroup Graphic Objects

1 Click . . . . *Drawing button*
on Standard toolbar to show Drawing toolbar.

2 Select . . . . *grouped objects to ungroup*

3 Click . . . . *Ungroup Objects button*

Set Properties of Graphic Objects

Sets objects to move and size with underlying cells or chart. Sets print property of object.

1 Select .... *graphic object(s)*

2 Click .... **Format**
then click .... **Object...** or **Selected Object...**

```
              FROM PROPERTIES
```

3 Select .... *Object Positioning option:*
Objects in worksheets:
Move and Size with Cells (default) — to move and size object with underlying cells.
Move but Don't Size with Cells — to move object with underlying cells.
Don't Move or Size with Cells — object is independent of underlying cells.
Objects in charts:
Size with chart, Do not size with chart

To enable or disable printing of object:

• Select or deselect .... ☐ **Print Object**

4 Click .... | OK |

Insert Graphic File (Picture)

Inserts a graphic file into Excel. The supported file formats (such as .BMP and .PCX) will depend upon the filters selected when you installed Excel. You can add or remove these filters by running Excel Setup.

1 Select .... *upper-left cell*
where graphic will be inserted.

OR

Enable (page 196) .... *chart editing*

2 Click .... **Insert, Picture...**

3 Select file in .... *Picture dialog box*

NOTE: *The features in the Picture dialog box are similar to the features in the Open dialog box (page 29). By default, Excel previews the graphic file you select in the Picture dialog box.*

4 Click .... | OK |

Copy a Picture of Cells, Graphic Objects, or Chart

NOTE: Pictures are not linked to the source data.

1 Select . . . . *cell(s)* or *object(s)* or *chart*
to copy as a picture.
NOTE: The chart can be on a sheet or an embedded chart.
If graphic objects are within the cells you select, they too will be copied.

2 Press <u>Shift</u> and click . . . . **Edit, Copy Picture...**

3 Select . . . . ○ **As Shown on <u>S</u>creen**
to copy selection as it currently appears on screen.

OR

Select . . . . ○ **As Shown when <u>P</u>rinted**
to copy selection as it would appear when printed.

4 Select . . . . ○ **Pic<u>t</u>ure**
NOTE: The Picture format ensures that you can view the image
on systems that have a different display type.

OR

Select . . . . ○ **Bitmap**

5 Click . . . . | OK |

6 Select . . . . *upper-left cell* or *object*
in worksheet to receive picture.

OR

Open . . . . *application to receive picture*

7 Click . . . . **Edit, <u>P</u>aste**

Include Graphic Objects in a Sort

Sort Rows

1 Size (page 188) . . . . *graphic objects*
so they are no taller than a single row.

2 Select . . . . *cells containing data and objects to sort*

3 Sort (page 126) . . . . *selection*

Sort Columns

1 Size (page 188) . . . . *graphic objects*
so they are no wider than a single column.

2 Select . . . . *cells containing data and objects to sort*

3 Sort (page 126) . . . . *selection*

Draw a Straight Line or Arrow

1 Click . . . . *Drawing button* 🔲
on Standard toolbar to show Drawing toolbar.

2 Click . . . . *Line button* ◻
   OR
   Click . . . . *Arrow button* ◻
   Pointer becomes a +

3 Position . . . . +
where line will begin.

To create line without constraints:

- Drag . . . . *line*
  until desired size and direction is obtained.

To create horizontal, vertical or 45 degree lines:

- Press <u>Shift</u> and drag . . . . *line*
  until desired size and direction is obtained.

To create a line and align it to nearest gridlines:

- Press <u>Alt</u> and drag . . . . *line*
  until desired size and direction is obtained.

Create a Chart

1 Select . . . . *cells containing data to plot*

2 Click . . . . **Insert, Chart ▶**

then click . . . . **On This Sheet** or **As New Sheet**

> **NOTE:** *You can also click the* 📊 *(ChartWizard button) on the Standard toolbar to create an embedded chart on the worksheet.*

If On This Sheet,
Pointer becomes a +₁₁₁

- Drag . . . . *chart outline to desired size*

> **NOTE:** *To create a square chart, press Shift while dragging chart outline. To align chart with cell structure, press Alt while dragging chart outline.*

– FROM CHARTWIZARD - STEP 1 OF 5 –

3 If necessary, select (in worksheet) or type
reference to cells to plot in . . . . **Range:** [   ]

4 Click . . . . [Next >]

– FROM CHARTWIZARD - STEP 2 OF 5 –

5 Click (page 205) . . . . *desired chart type*

6 Click . . . . [Next >]

– FROM CHARTWIZARD - STEP 3 OF 5 –

7 Click . . . . *desired format for chart type*

– FROM CHARTWIZARD - STEP 4 OF 5 –

8 Select . . . . *chart options:*

To change how to plot data series:

- Select . . . . ○ **Rows** or ○ **Columns**

  Excel shows the result of your selections in sample chart.

To specify rows or columns to use for axis labels, legend text or chart title:

- Select number of rows/columns in . . . **Use First:** [⬍]

  > **NOTE:** *Options will depend on chart type. To plot values in first row or column (not use them as labels) select 0 (zero).*

9 Click . . . . [Next >]

Continued ...

Create a Chart (continued)

— FROM CHARTWIZARD - STEP 5 OF 5 —

10 Select . . . . *other chart options:*

To add or remove legend:

- Select . . . . ○ **Y̲es** or ○ **N̲o**

To add a chart title:

- Type title in . . . . **C̲hart Title:** [   ]

To add axis titles:

- Type titles in . . . . *provided Axis Titles boxes*
  NOTE: Available options will depend on chart type.

11 Click . . . . [**F̲inish**]

Identify Chart Items

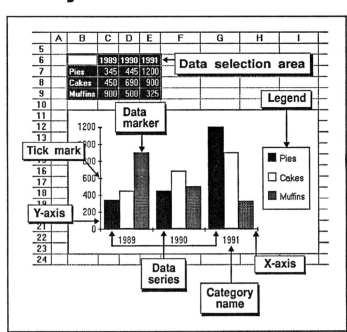

Sample Chart

Illustrated chart items:

- The **data selection area** is a selected range of worksheet cells containing data to plot in a chart.

- A **data marker** (S1P1, S1P2...) is a single symbol or shape in a chart representing one value from the data selection area.

- A **data series** (S1, S2...) is a group of related values in the same row or column in the data selection area. In a chart, the data series is represented by data markers that have the same pattern or color.

- **Category names** are classifications in which data values for each data series are compared.

- The **X-axis** is the horizontal line on which categories of data are usually plotted.

- The **Y-axis** is the vertical line on which data values are usually plotted

- A **tick mark** is a small line on an axis representing a scaled value or a change in categories.

- A **legend** is a box displaying labels for each data series, and the patterns, symbols or colors of data markers in each data series.

Chart items not illustrated:

- **3-D floor**, **walls** and **corners** are plot boundaries formed by the X, Y and Z axes of a 3-D chart.

- **Chart lines** are optional lines that include drop-lines, gridlines, hi-lo lines, series lines, trendlines and up/down lines. These lines can make it easier to read data values or the relationships between values in a chart.

- **Chart text** is text that describes a chart item. Examples of chart text include the chart title, axes labels, tick labels on an axis, and data marker and category name labels.

- **Error bars** express error amounts relative to each of the data markers in a data series. These bars are used primarily when plotting statistical data.

- **Graphic objects** are items, such as arrows and text boxes, that you can add to any location in the chart to emphasize data.

- The **chart area** is the space inside the chart that includes all items in the chart.

- The **plot area** is the space in which chart axes and data markers are drawn.

Enable Chart Editing

Edit an Embedded Chart

- Double-click . . . . **embedded chart**
  The chart is surrounded by a thick border with handles; if the entire chart was not displayed on the sheet, the chart appears in a window.

Edit a Chart Sheet

- Select . . . . **chart sheet**

A Chart toolbar may appear with these common chart buttons.

 Chart Type

 Default Chart

 ChartWizard

| **Horizontal Gridlines**

| **Legend**

Chart Edit Mode Features

Menu bar options

Excel also modifies the menu bar so options specific to the chart type and selected chart item are available. For example:

| Insert menu | Titles..., Data Labels..., Legend, Axes..., Gridlines... Picture..., Trendline..., Error Bars..., New Data... |
| Format menu | Selected Object..., Chart Type..., Auto Format..., 3-D View... |

Shortcut menu options

Excel will display the following shortcut menu items appropriate to the part of the chart you right-click on:

Clear	Clear selected item.
Insert:	Axes, Data Labels, Error Bars, Gridlines, Titles, Trendline.
Format:	Axis, Axis Title, Chart Area, Chart Title, Data Labels, Data Point, Data Series, Error Bars, Gridlines, Legend, Legend Entry, Legend Key, Trendline.

Chart Type, Autoformat, 3-D View, Format Chart Type Group

Name box

Excel displays the selected chart item in the Name box on the left side of the formula bar.

Select Chart Items

Typically, you will select chart items prior to selecting commands that act on the chart item in some way.

NOTE: *Excel marks the currently selected chart item with squares, and displays its name in the Name box.*

- Double-click . . . . *embedded chart*

OR

- Select . . . . *chart sheet*

To select next or previous class of chart items:

- Press . . . . 〔↑↓〕

To select next or previous subitem for selected chart class:

- Press . . . . 〔←→〕

To select a specific chart item with mouse:

- Click . . . . *chart item*

  Select a data series

  - Click . . . . *any data marker in data series*

  Select a data marker

  - Click . . . . *any data marker in data series*
    then click . . . . *data marker in selected series*

  Select chart area

  - Click . . . . *any blank area outside plot area*

  Select plot area

  - Click . . . . *any blank area inside plot area*

  Select a legend or legend subitems

  NOTE: *Legend subitems are the legend entry and key.*

  - Click . . . . *legend*
    then click . . . . *subitem in legend*

To deselect a selected chart item:

- Press . . . . 〔Esc〕

Change Range of Data to Plot

1 Enable (page 196) . . . . *chart editing*

2 Click . . . . *ChartWizard button* 📊
on Standard toolbar.

3 Select (in worksheet) or type
reference to data to plot in . . . . **Range:** [＿＿＿＿]

4 Click . . . . [<u>F</u>inish]

Change Orientation of Data Series to Rows or Columns

1 Enable (page 196) . . . . *chart editing*

2 Click . . . . *ChartWizard button* 📊
on Standard toolbar.

3 Click . . . . [Next >]

4 Select . . . . ◯ **<u>R</u>ows** or ◯ **<u>C</u>olumns**

5 Click . . . . [OK]

Change How Rows or Columns in Plot Area are Used in Chart Text

*Depending on the chart type, you can use this procedure to change
axis labels, legend entries and the chart title based on text in the plot area.*

1 Enable (page 196) . . . . *chart editing*

2 Click . . . . *ChartWizard button* 📊
on Standard toolbar.

3 Click . . . . [Next >]

4 Select number of rows/columns in . . . . . **Use First:** [＿＿] ⬍

*NOTE: Options will depend on chart type. To not use values
in first row or column as labels (plot the values instead), select 0 (zero).*

5 Click . . . . [OK]

Add Data to Embedded Chart

Adds data in a range of cells to an embedded chart.

1 Select . . . . *range of data to add to chart*
   NOTE: *Include category or data series names.*

2 Point to . . . . *border of selection*
   Pointer becomes a 🖑

3 Drag . . . . *border outline onto chart*

   If Paste Special dialog box appears,

   a Select options appropriate to your chart and the selection.

   b Click . . . . | OK |

   NOTE: *If you make the wrong choices in the Paste Special dialog box, select Undo from the Edit menu.*

Add Data to Chart Sheet

Adds data in a range of cells to a chart sheet.

1 Select . . . . *range of data to add to chart*
   NOTE: *Include category or data series names.*

2 Click . . . . **Edit, Copy**

3 Select . . . . **chart sheet**

4 Click . . . . **Edit, Paste**

   If Paste Special dialog box appears,

   a Select options appropriate to your chart and the selection.

   b Click . . . . | OK |

   NOTE: *If you make the wrong choices in the Paste Special dialog box, select Undo from the Edit menu.*

5 Press . . . . **Esc**
   to end copy.

Add Data to Embedded Chart or Chart Sheet

Adds data in non-adjacent cells to a chart.

1 Enable (page 196) . . . . ***chart editing***

2 Click . . . . **Insert, New Data...**

3 Select (in worksheet) or type
reference to cells containing data to add in . **Range:** [   ]
NOTE: *Include category or data series names.*

If Paste Special dialog box appears,

a Select options appropriate to your chart and the selection.

b Click . . . . [OK]
NOTE: *If you make the wrong choices in the Paste Special dialog box, select Undo from the Edit menu.*

Change Chart Type ▶ Using Toolbar

Changes the chart type for an entire chart or a selected data series.
When you change the chart type for a selected series, you are creating a combination chart.

1 Enable (page 196) . . . . ***chart editing***

If changing chart type for a <u>data series</u>,

• Select . . . . ***data series***

2 Click . . . . **Chart Type arrow** [📊±]
on Chart toolbar.

3 Click . . . . ***picture of desired chart type***

Change Chart Type ▶ Using Menu

*Changes the chart type for an entire chart, a selected data series or a
chart type group (one or more data series formatted as one chart type).
When you change the chart type for a selected series, you are creating
a combination or overlay chart.*

1 Enable (page 196) . . . . *chart editing*

To change chart type for a <u>data series</u>:
- Select . . . . *data series*

2 Click . . . . **F**ormat, Chart **T**ype...

To change chart type for selected <u>data series</u>:
- Select . . . . ○ **Selected Series**

To change chart type for previously created <u>group</u>:
a Select . . . . ○ **Group:**

b Select group to change in . . . . **Group:** list

To change chart type for <u>entire chart</u>:
- Select . . . . ○ **Entire Chart**

3 Select . . . . ○ **2-D** or ○ **3-D**

4 Click . . . . *desired chart type*

To select a chart subtype (style):
a Click . . . . | Options... |

⌐ *FROM SUBTYPE* ⌐

b Select picture of subtype in . . . . **Subtype** group

5 Click . . . . | OK |

Format a Chart Type Group

NOTE: By default, charts contain a single chart type group in which each data series is formatted in the same way. When you change a chart type (pages 200 and 201) for a data series, Excel creates a chart type group for that series. A chart with more than one chart group is often called a combination or overlay chart. When you plot data along a secondary axis (page 202), Excel also creates a chart type group for that series.

1 Enable (page 196) . . . . *chart editing*

2 a Click . . . . **Fo**rmat

   b Click . . . . *numbered chart type group*
       at bottom of menu.

To plot group on primary or secondary axis:
(For charts containing more than one group)

> FROM **AXIS**

- Select . . . . . ◯ **P**rimary Axis or ◯ **S**econdary Axis

To select format options for chart type group:

> FROM **OPTIONS**

- Select . . . . **Format options for group:**
  Overlap, Gap Width, Series Lines, Vary Colors By Point/Slice,
  Drop Lines, High-Low, Up-Down Bars, Radar Axis Labels,
  Angle of First Slice, Hole Size, Chart Type command, Gap Depth (3-D),
  Chart Depth (3-D), Vary Colors by Point (3-D)

To change order of series in chart type group:

> FROM **SERIES ORDER**

a Select name of series in . . . . **S**eries Order: *list*

b Click . . . . | Move **U**p | or | Move **D**own |

To change subtype (style) for chart type group:

> FROM **SUBTYPE**

- Select picture of subtype in . . . . **S**ubtype group

3 Click . . . . | OK |

Use Picture as Data Markers

Uses graphics, created in other applications or Excel, as data markers for the following chart types: 2-D Bar, 2-D Column, Line, Radar, and XY (Scatter) charts.

1 From source application (i.e., Paint or Excel), create, open, or insert graphic file.

2 Select . . . . **graphic object**
to use as a data marker.

3 Click . . . . **Edit, Copy**
to copy image to Clipboard.

4 If source of object is another application, select . . . . **Excel**

5 Enable (page 196) . . . . **chart editing**

6 Select . . . . **data series** or **data marker**
to replace with picture.

7 Click . . . . **Paste button**
on Standard toolbar.

NOTE: *To format picture, see Format Chart Items, page 216.*

Clear Picture Markers

1 Enable (page 196) . . . . **chart editing**

2 Select . . . . **data series** or **data marker**
to clear picture from.

3 Click . . . . **Edit, Clear ▸, Formats**

Auto-Format a Chart

Applies a built-in or custom-made format to a chart.

1 Enable (page 196) . . . . *chart editing*

2 Click . . . . **F_ormat, A_utoFormat...**

3 Click . . . . ◯ **B_uilt-in** or ◯ **U_ser-Defined**

4 Select format name in . . . . **G_alleries** or **F_ormats** *list*
Galleries list items include: Area, Bar, Column, Line, Pie,
Doughnut, Radar, XY (Scatter), Combination, 3-D Area, 3-D Bar,
3-D Column, 3-D Line, 3-D Pie, 3-D Surface

If applying a built-in format,

- Select picture of format in . . . . **F_ormats:** *group*

5 Click . . . . | OK |

Create or Delete a Custom Auto-Format

1 Enable (page 196) . . . . *chart editing*

2 Format . . . . *chart as desired*

3 Click . . . . **F_ormat, A_utoFormat...**

4 Click . . . . ◯ **U_ser-Defined**

5 Click . . . . | Custo_mize... |

To add a custom format:

a Click . . . . | _Add... |

b Type name for custom format in . . **F_ormat Name:** | |

c Type description in . . . . **D_escription:** | |

d Click . . . . | OK |

To delete a custom format:

a Select format to delete in . . . . **F_ormats:** *list*

b Click . . . . | _Delete |

c Click . . . . | OK |

6 Click . . . . | Close |

Guide for Selecting a Chart Type

When plotting   **select this chart type**

- relative values over a period of time . . . . **Area**
- to emphasize amount of change in values . . . . **Area**
- categories on Y axis . . . . **Bar**
- to compare values of items . . . . **Bar**
- values of items and relation to whole . . . . **Stacked Bar**
- changing values for same item at specific times . . . . . **Column**
- categories on Y axis . . . . **Column**
- to compare items on X axis . . . . **Column**
- values at specific times and relation to whole . **Stacked Column**
- trends . . . . **Line**
- values at regular intervals . . . . **Line**
- to emphasize rate of change . . . . **Line**
- to emphasize time flow . . . . **Line**
- stock prices . . . . **Line** (Subtype--High-Low-Close)
                                  Line (Subtype--Open-High-Low-Close)
  (Order of data series must correspond to name of chart)
- relation of values to a whole . . . . **Pie**
- one data series . . . . **Pie**
- relation of more than one data series to a whole . . . **Doughnut**
- values at unrelated intervals . . . . **XY (Scatter)**
- relationships between numerous values . . . . **XY (Scatter)**
- scientific data . . . . **XY (Scatter)**
- best combination for two sets of data . . . . **3-D Surface**
- relationships between large amounts of data . . . . **3-D Surface**

NOTE: *Use 3-D versions of chart types for emphasis and visual appeal:*
3-D Area, 3-D Bar Chart, 3-D Column, 3-D Perspective Column,
3-D Line, 3-D Pie, 3-D Surface

Return Chart to Default Chart Type and Format

The default chart type is the column type with a legend.

1 Enable (page 196) . . . . ***chart editing***

2 Click . . . . ***Default Chart button*** 🖼
on Chart toolbar.

Set Default Chart Options

NOTE: *Options will depend upon chart type, and if the chart is embedded or on a chart sheet.*

1 Enable (page 196) . . . . ***chart editing***

2 Click . . . . **T̲ools, Options...**

╭──────────── *FROM CHART* ────────────╮

To set how empty cells are plotted in Line charts:

● Select . . . . ***Empty Cells Plotted as option:***
  N̲ot Plotted (leave gaps) *— to leave gaps in lines when cells are empty.*
  Z̲ero *— to treat blank cells as zero.*
  I̲nterpolated *— to fill in for empty cells with connected lines.*

To set plotting of visible cells:

● Select or deselect . . . . ☐ **P̲lot Visible Cells Only**

To set chart sizing with window frame:

● Select or deselect . . ☐ **C̲hart Sizes with Window Frame**

To change default chart:

● Select chart type in . . **D̲efault Chart Format:** [　　　　▼]
  NOTE: *Select Built-in to reset chart to original default type.*

To make current chart type the default chart:

a Click . . . . [U̲se the Current Chart...]

b Type format name in . . . . **F̲ormat Name:** [　　　]

c Click . . . . [OK]

3 Click . . . . [OK]

Display or Hide Axes

1 Enable (page 196) . . . . *chart editing*

2 Click . . . . _I_nsert, A_x_es...

3 Select or deselect . . . . ☐ _C_ategory (X) Axis

AND/OR

Select or deselect . . . . ☐ _V_alue (Y) Axis

If chart is a 3-D chart,

- Select or deselect . . . . *Primary Axis options:*
  _C_ategory (X) Axis, _S_eries (Y) Axis, _V_alue (Z) Axis

4 Click . . . . | OK |

Change Scale on an Axis

For _category_ axes,
- *sets where (X) axis will cross (Y) axis;*
- *sets number of categories between tick mark labels;*
- *sets number of categories between each pair of tick marks;*
- *other options — Value (Y) Axis Crosses Between Categories, Categories
  in Reverse Order, Value (Y) Axis Crosses at Maximum Category.*

For _series_ axes (value axis),
- *sets minimum and maximum data values displayed on axes;*
- *sets increments between tick marks and gridlines;*
- *sets where (X) axis will cross (Y) axis;*
- *other options — Logarithmic Scale, Values in Reverse Order,
  Category (X) Axis Crosses at Maximum Value.*

1 Enable (page 196) . . . . *chart editing*

2 Double-click . . . . *axis*

> FROM **SCALE**

3 Select options appropriate to selected axis and chart type.

4 Click . . . . | OK |

Insert Data Labels

Adds data labels to a data series or a specific data marker in a chart.

1 Enable (page 196) . . . . *chart editing*

2 Select (page 197) . . . . *data series* or *data marker*
to which label(s) will be added.

OR

Select . . . . *chart or plot area*
to add labels to all data markers.

3 Click . . . . Insert, Data Labels...

4 Select . . . . *Data Labels option:*
None – to remove existing data label.
Show Value – to show value of data point.
Show Percent – to show percentage of part to whole for pie and
doughnut charts.
Show Label – to show category or series name.
Show Label and Percent – to show category or series name and
percentage of part to whole for pie and doughnut charts.

To display legend keys next to data labels:

- Select . . . . ☐ **Show Legend Key next to Label**

5 Click . . . . | OK |

NOTE: Data labels are linked to worksheet data, and
they can be edited in the worksheet (page 209), edited
in the chart (page 209), formatted (pages 214 and 216),
and moved (page 218).

Insert Chart Title and Axes Labels

1 Enable (page 196) . . . . *chart editing*

2 Click . . . . Insert, Titles...

3 Select . . . . *Attach Text to options:*
Options may include: *Chart Title, Value (Y) Axis, Value (Z) Axis,*
Category (X) Axis, Second Value (Y) Axis, Second Category (X) Axis,
Series (Y) Axis

4 Click . . . . | OK |

NOTE: Chart titles and axes labels are not linked to worksheet
data, and they can be edited in the chart (page 209),
formatted (pages 214 and 216), and moved (page 218).

Edit Chart Text in Chart

With this procedure, you can edit unlinked chart text (such as axis and chart titles, text boxes, and trendline labels) and some linked text (data labels and tick mark labels).

NOTE: *When you edit linked text, Excel removes the link to the worksheet data.*

1 Enable (page 196) . . . . *chart editing*

2 Select . . . . *chart item containing text*

To replace existing text with new text:

a Type . . . . *new text*
Text appears in formula bar.

b Enter . . . . 🔲

To edit existing text:

a Click . . . . *desired character position in chart item*

b Insert and delete . . . . *characters as desired*

c Click . . . . *anywhere outside of chart item*

Edit Linked Chart Text in Worksheet

When you edit linked text (legend entries, data labels (values or text), and tick mark labels) in the worksheet, Excel automatically updates the chart.

1 Select . . . . *worksheet containing chart data*

2 Edit . . . . *cell containing data label or value*

3 Enter . . . . 🔲

Change Data Label Options

1 Enable (page 196) . . . . ***chart editing***

2 Double-click . . . . ***data series*** or ***data marker***

> *FROM DATA LABELS*

To relink data labels to worksheet cells:

● Select . . . . ☐ **Automatic Text**
   *NOTE: This option is available only if you edited
   text in a data label for the data series or marker.*

To show or hide legend key:

● Select or deselect. . ☐ **Show Legend Key next to Label**

3 Click . . . . `OK`

Link Chart Text to Worksheet Data

*Chart text, such as legend entries, data labels, and tick mark labels, are
automatically linked to the contents of cells in a worksheet. You can use
this procedure to link other chart text (such as axis labels, chart titles,
text box text) to worksheet cells.*

1 Enable (page 196) . . . . ***chart editing***

2 Select . . . . ***chart item containing unlinked text***

3 Press . . . . 🔲
   Equal sign appears in formula bar.

4 Select (in worksheet) or type . . . . ***reference to cell***
   containing text.

5 Enter . . . . ⤶

Insert a Legend

1 Enable (page 196) . . . . *chart editing*

2 Click . . . . **Insert, Legend**

   OR

   Click . . . . *Legend button* 🖽
   on Chart toolbar.

   NOTE: *Legend entries are linked to worksheet data, and they
   can be edited in the worksheet (page 209) or in the chart (see below).
   Legend, legend entries, and keys can be formatted (pages 214 and
   216). You can also move (page 218) and size (page 218) the legend.*

Edit Legend Entry in Chart

NOTE: *You can also edit legend entries in the worksheet (page 209).*

1 Enable (page 196) . . . . *chart editing*

2 Double-click . . . . *data series for legend to change*

┌─────── FROM NAME AND VALUES ───────┐

3 Select reference (in worksheet) containing
   series name or type series name in . . . . . . **Name:** [   ]
   NOTE: *If you type a name, the automatic link to the
   worksheet is ended.*

4 Click . . . . [OK]

Insert or Remove Gridlines

1 Enable (page 196) . . . . *chart editing*

2 Click . . . . *Horizontal Gridlines button* 🖽
   on Chart toolbar.

   OR

   a Click . . . . **Insert, Gridlines...**

   b Select or deselect . . . . *Gridlines options*
      NOTE: *Options depend on chart type.*

   c Click . . . . [OK]

Insert or Modify Error Bars

Error bars express error amounts relative to each of the data markers in a data series. These bars are used primarily when plotting statistical data.

1 Enable (page 196) . . . . **chart editing**

2 Select . . . . **data series to receive error bars**

3 Click . . . . **Insert, Error Bars...**

```
         ┌──── FROM Y ERROR BARS ────┐
─────────┘                            └─────────
```

4 Select . . . . **Display option:**
Both, Plus, Minus, None

5 Select . . . . **Error Amount option:**
Fixed Value, Percentage, Standard Deviation(s), Standard Error, Custom

NOTE: *If working with an XY (Scatter) chart, you can also insert or change x error bars.*

6 Click . . . . | OK |

Change 3-D Walls and Gridlines to 2-D

NOTE: *Chart type must be a 3-D Bar or Column.*

1 Enable (page 196) . . . . **chart editing**

2 Click . . . . **Insert, Gridlines...**

3 Select . . . . ☐ **2-D Walls and Gridlines**

4 Click . . . . | OK |

Insert Trendlines

1 Enable (page 196) . . . . *chart editing*

2 Select . . . . *data series to plot trend for*

3 Click . . . . **Insert, Trendline...**

FROM TYPE

4 Select trend type in . . . . **Trend/Regression Type** *group*
Trend types include: Linear, Logarithmic, Polynomial, Power, Exponential, Moving Average

If Polynomial,

- Type or select highest power
  for independent variable in . . . . **Order:** ⊞

If Moving Average,

- Type or select number of periods
  for calculation in . . . . **Period:** ⊞

5 Click . . . . | OK |

Delete Chart Item

1 Enable (page 196) . . . . *chart editing*

2 Select . . . . *chart item to delete*

3 Press . . . . **Del**
NOTE: *If you delete the wrong items, select Undo Clear from the Edit menu.*

Other Items You Can Insert in a Chart

You can add graphic objects, pictures and unattached text boxes to any chart.

Format Chart Text

Changes font and alignment of selected text or all text in chart item.

1 Enable (page 196) . . . . *chart editing*

2 Double-click . . . . *chart text* or *legend*
to format entire text.

OR

a Select . . . . *chart item*
to format individual characters.
*NOTE: You cannot format individual characters if the text
(i.e., legend text) is linked to worksheet data.*

b Select . . . . *characters in text to format*

c Click . . . . *Format, Selected . . .*

FROM *FONT*

• Select (page 150) . . . . *Font options*

FROM *ALIGNMENT*

• Select (page 146) . . . . *Alignment options*
(Not available for character formatting).

3 Click . . . . [OK]
*NOTE: You can also format selected text or text in a selected chart
item by clicking the desired format buttons on the Formatting toolbar.*

Rotate and Elevate a
3-D Chart ▶ by Dragging

1 Enable (page 196) . . . . *chart editing*

2 Select . . . . *any 3-D corner*

3 Point to . . . . *any corner*
Pointer becomes a ┼

4 Drag . . . . *chart outline*
until desired view is obtained.
*NOTE: To view data markers as you drag, hold down Ctrl while
dragging corner.*

Set View Options for a 3-D Chart ▸ Using Menu

1 Enable (page 196) . . . . *chart editing*

2 Click . . . . **Format, 3-D View...**

To increase or decrease elevation:

- Click . . . . *Elevation buttons* ⬆ or ⬇

To rotate chart left or right:

- Click . . . . *Rotation buttons* ↺ or ↻

To increase or decrease perspective:
(Not available if Right Angle Axes is selected.)

- Click . . *Perspective buttons* ⬇ or ⬆

To lock axes at right angles:

- Select . . . . ☐ **Right Angle Axes**

To scale chart to fill window:
(Available if Right Angle Axes is selected.)

- Select . . . . ☐ **Auto Scaling**

To set height in relation to base of chart:

- Type number (5-500) in . . . . **Height:** [　　] **% of Base**

To preview chart in sheet with current settings:

a Move . . . . *dialog box so that chart is visible*

b Click . . . . [Apply]

To return chart to default settings:

- Click . . . . [Default]

3 Click . . . . [OK]

Format Chart Numbers

1 Enable (page 196) . . . . *chart editing*

2 Double-click . . . . *chart item containing values*

> FROM NUMBER

3 Select a category in . . . . **<u>C</u>ategory:** *list*
Categories include: General, Number, Currency, Accounting, Date, Time, Percentage, Fraction, Scientific, Text, Special, Custom

4 Select option(s) for selected category.

To link data labels containing values to worksheet data:

• Select . . . . ☐ **<u>L</u>inked to Source**

5 Click . . . . | OK |

Format Chart Items

Formats the following chart items: axis, 3-D floor, 3-D walls, borders, lines, chart area, data series, data markers, error bars, gridlines, legend, legend key, picture markers, plot area, tick marks, and trendlines.

1 Enable (page 196) . . . . *chart editing*

2 Double-click . . . . *chart item to format*

> FROM PATTERNS

NOTE: *Options will depend on the chart item you double clicked.*

To format <u>border</u>:

• Select . . . . **Border options:**
<u>A</u>utomatic, <u>N</u>one, Custom (<u>S</u>tyle, <u>C</u>olor, <u>W</u>eight), Sha<u>d</u>ow

To format <u>area</u>:

• Select . . . . **Area options:**
<u>A</u>utomatic, No<u>n</u>e, Co<u>l</u>or, <u>P</u>attern, In<u>v</u>ert if Negative

To format <u>axis</u>:

• Select . . . . **Axis option:**
<u>A</u>utomatic, <u>N</u>one, Custom (<u>S</u>tyle, <u>C</u>olor, <u>W</u>eight)

Continued ...

Format Chart Items (continued)

To format <u>tick marks</u>:

- Select . . . . *Tick-Mark Labels option:*
  N<u>o</u>ne, <u>L</u>ow, Hi<u>g</u>h, Ne<u>x</u>t to Axis

  AND/OR

  Select . . . . *Tick Mark Type options:*
  M<u>aj</u>or (None, Inside, Outside, Cross),
  Mino<u>r</u> (None, Inside, Outside, Cross)

To format <u>line</u>:

- Select . . . . *Line options:*
  <u>A</u>utomatic, <u>N</u>one, Custom (<u>S</u>tyle, <u>C</u>olor, <u>W</u>eight), S<u>m</u>oothed Line

To format <u>markers</u>:

- Select . . . . *Marker options:*
  A<u>u</u>tomatic, N<u>o</u>ne, Custom (Styl<u>e</u>, <u>F</u>oreground, <u>B</u>ackground)

To format <u>picture markers</u>:

- Select . . . . *Picture Format option:*
  St<u>r</u>etch, St<u>a</u>ck, Stack and S<u>c</u>ale to (<u>U</u>nits/Picture)

3 Click . . . . | OK |

Delete an Embedded Chart

1 Click . . . . *embedded chart*
Handles appear on chart border.

2 Press . . . . |Del|

Delete a Chart Sheet

*(See **Delete Sheets**, page 45.)*

Size or Move an Embedded Chart or Chart Item

(See Size Graphic Objects, page 188.)
(See Move Graphic Objects, page 188.)

Protect Embedded Chart

(See Protect a Sheet, page 181.)
(See Lock Cells or Graphic Objects, page 182.)

Protect a Chart Sheet

(See Protect a Workbook, page 180.
See Protect a Sheet, page 181.)

Size a Chart's Plot Area or Legend

1 Enable (page 196) . . . . *chart editing*

2 Select . . . . *plot area* or *legend*
  Handles appear on item's border.

3 Point to . . . . *handle on side of item to size*
  Pointer becomes a ↘ ↔ ↗ ↕

4 Drag . . . . *item outline in direction to size*

Move a Chart Item

You can move the plot area, legend, chart title, data labels, and axes labels.

1 Enable (page 196) . . . . *chart editing*

2 Select . . . . *chart item to move*

3 Drag . . . . *chart item outline*

Size a Data Marker to Change a Plotted Value

Changes the value in the chart and the worksheet for the following 2-D chart types: Bar, Column, Line, Pie, and Stacked, as well as Doughnut and XY (Scatter) charts.

1 Enable (page 196) . . . . *chart editing*

2 Select . . . . *data marker*
representing value to change.

3 Point to . . . . *largest handle of data marker*
Pointer becomes a $\updownarrow$ or $+$

4 Drag . . . . *marker outline up or down*
Excel displays the value in the Name box.

If marker represents a value that is based on a formula,
The Goal Seek dialog box appears.

   a Select (in worksheet) reference
     to cell that will change in . . **By <u>c</u>hanging cell:** [＿＿＿]

   b Click . . . . [OK]

   c Click . . . . [OK]

Position Legend in Chart

1 Enable (page 196) . . . . *chart editing*

2 Right-click . . . . *legend*

3 Click . . . . **Format Legend...**

FROM PLACEMENT

4 Select . . . . *Type option:*
Bottom, <u>C</u>orner, <u>T</u>op, <u>R</u>ight, <u>L</u>eft.

5 Click . . . . [OK]

Insert and Use a Data Map

1 Select . . . . *cells containing geographic data*

2 Click . . . . **Insert, Map...**
Pointer becomes a ┼

3 Drag . . . . *rectangle to define map area*

4 a If prompted, select desired map in . . . . *list*

   b Click . . . . | OK |

The *Data Map Control window (below) opens and the*
Data Map toolbar (next page) appears below the menu bar.

Sample Data Map Control Window

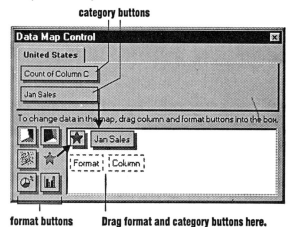

category buttons

format buttons   **Drag format and category buttons here.**

Data Map Control Window Options

To:	Procedure:
Add or replace a data format	Drag **format button** onto a Format area or format button you wish to replace in box. Format buttons include: Value Shading, Category Shading, Dot Density, Graduated Symbol, Pie Chart, Column Chart.
Assign a data category to a data format	Drag **category button** (in top area) onto format button you have added to the box.
Remove data from map	Drag desired category button out of the box.
Set options for data category/format buttons	Double-click either button in the box to change format or set summary function and value ranges in map.

Insert and Use a Data Map (continued)

Data Map Toolbar Options

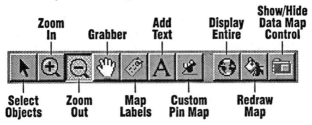

Toolbar Buttons	How to Use Selected Toolbar Button
Add Text	Click in map, type desired text, then press Enter.
Custom Pin Map	Create or edit *custom pin maps* (labeled markers that point out areas of interest in map). If prompted, type name for new pin map or select existing pin map name in list, then click OK. Click where you want a marker, type label, and press Enter. To format a marker, right-click it and select Format.
Display Entire	Shows entire map.
Grabber	Drag hand icon over map to move desired area of map into view.
Map Labels	Select map feature to label in list, then select Create labels from option (Map feature names or Values from). Click OK. Point to area in map to label (Excel shows the label). Click to add the label.
Redraw Map	Redraws map.
Select Objects	Click object to select in map. You can move or size selected object. To edit a text object, click it a second time, then type or edit text.
Show/Hide Data Map Controls	Shows or hides Data Map Control window.
Zoom In	Click area of map to magnify.
Zoom Out	Click in map to show more of the map.

Insert and Use a Data Map (continued)

Data Map Menu Commands

NOTE: This table lists only menus containing Data Map features.

Menu	Menu Items
View	Data Map Control— Show or hide Data Map Control window.
	Toolbar — Show or hide Data Map toolbar.
	Title — Show or hide map title.
	Subtitle — Show or hide map subtitle.
	All Legends — Show all legends.
	Entire Map — Show entire map (removes zoom).
	Previous — Show previous zoom view.
	Redraw Map — Redraw map.
Insert	Data — Select in worksheet cells containing data to add to map.
	External Data — Select in Open Database dialog box a database file containing data to add to map. Click Open and follow prompts.
Tools	Labeler — Select map feature to label in list, then select Create labels from option (Map feature names or Values from). Click OK. Point to area in map to label (Excel shows label). Click to add the label.
	Options — Select Map Matching options (Quick, Thorough), Feature Sizing Units (Inches, Centimeters, Millimeters), and Compact Legends by Default option.
Map	Features — Add/remove, show/hide map features (such as US Highways); customize visible map features.
	Add Feature — Select feature in list to add to map.
	Save Map Template — Select Save current options (Map features, View) and enter name for template. When you create a new map, this map will appear in list of maps.
	Delete Map Template — Select map template to delete in list.
	Refresh — Update map to show changes to map data in worksheet.
	Open Custom Pin Map — Select existing custom pin map in list.
	Close Custom Pin Map — Remove custom pin map markers from map.
	Delete Custom Pin Map — Select name of custom pin map to delete in list.
	Format Options — Select format options for map features (such as Value Shading or Dot Density). Select summary function and value range.

Insert and Use a Data Map (continued)

Data Map Right-Click Options

Item in Map	Shortcut Menu Items
Map area	Features — Add/remove, show/hide map features (such as US Highways); customize visible map features.
	Add Feature — Add feature to map.
	Save Map Template — Save current map features and view. When you create a new map, this map will appear in list of maps.
	Refresh — Update map to show changes in worksheet.
Text	Clear — Delete item.
	Format Font — Set font attributes of text.
Pin map marker	Clear — Delete pin marker.
	Format — Format pin marker (symbol and font).
Legend	Hide — Hide legend. (You can show legend again by selecting View, All Legends.)
	Edit — Edit legend text, font, currency format, and legend entries.
	Compact — Switch between showing compact or enlarged legend information.

Enable Data Map Editing

- Double-click . . . . ***data map***
  The Data Map Control window (page 220) opens and the Data Map toolbar (page 221) appears below the menu bar.

To update map to show changes to source data:

- Click . . . . ***Map Refresh button*** 🔲
  in upper left corner of map.

Insert New Embedded OLE Object in Worksheet

*Inserts a copy of data as an embedded object into Excel. An **object** is a collection of information created with an OLE object application such as Word.*

1 Select . . . . ***cell where object will be inserted***

2 Click . . . . <u>I</u>nsert, <u>O</u>bject...

*FROM **CREATE NEW***

3 Select object type to create in . . . . <u>O</u>bject Type: *list*

To display inserted object as an icon:

• Select . . . . ☐ Displa<u>y</u> as Icon

4 Click . . . . | OK |

If object workspace appears in worksheet,
(The source application, such as Word, now provides menus and tools.)

a Use tools provided to create the object in-place.

b Click . . . . ***in worksheet***
to deselect object and return to normal editing.
Menus and tools from Excel reappear.

If object appears as an icon,
(Source application opens in a separate window and icon appears ghosted in Excel worksheet.)

a Use tools provided to create the object.

b Click . . . . <u>F</u>ile, E<u>x</u>it & Return to . . .

c Click . . . . ***in worksheet***
to deselect object and return to normal editing.

Embed Portion of Existing OLE Object into Worksheet

1 Open .... *application containing object to embed*
NOTE: *Application must support object linking and embedding, such as Paint.*

2 Select .... *part of document to embed*

3 Click .... **Edit, Copy**

4 Select .... *Excel application*

5 Select .... *cell where object will be inserted*

6 Click .... **Edit, Paste Special...**

7 Select .... ○ **Paste:**

8 Select format of object in .... **As:** *list*

To display object as an icon:

- Select .... ☐ **Display as Icon**

   To change icon:

   a Click .... | Change Icon... |

   b Select icon in .... **Icon:** *list*
   NOTE: *You can click the Browse button to select another source file (i.e., MORICONS.DLL) for the icon.*

   c If desired, edit caption in .... **Caption:** [   ]

   d Click .... | OK |

9 Click .... | OK |

Insert Existing File as Embedded OLE Object

Inserts a copy of existing file as an embedded object into current worksheet.
*An **object** is a collection of information created with an OLE **object**
application, such as Paint, that you can embed into a **container**
application, such as Excel.*

1 Select . . . . *cell where object will be inserted*

2 Click . . . . **I**nsert, **O**bject...

FROM CREATE FROM FILE

3 Type path and file name in . . . . **File N̲ame:** [   ]
   OR
   a Click . . . . [B̲rowse...]
   b Use Browse dialog box to insert the file.

To display object as an icon:

   • Select . . . . ☐ **Displ̲ay as Icon**

4 Click . . . . [OK]
   The object or object icon appears in the worksheet.

5 Click . . . . *in worksheet*
   to deselect object and return to normal editing.
   *(Also see **Edit OLE Objects**, page 228.)*

Insert Existing File as Linked OLE Object

Inserts a link to an existing file as a linked object into current worksheet.
*An **object** is a collection of information created with an OLE **object***
application**, such as Paint, that you can embed into a **container
***application**, such as Excel. Changes made to the source object will*
automatically change the object in the worksheet and other documents
to which the object is linked.

1 Select . . . . ***cell where object will be inserted***

2 Click . . . . <u>I</u>nsert, <u>O</u>bject...

> *FROM CREATE FROM FILE*

3 Type path and file name in . . . . File <u>N</u>ame: [   ]

   OR

   a Click . . . . [<u>B</u>rowse...]

   b Use Browse dialog box to insert the file.

4 Select . . . . ☐ <u>L</u>ink to File

To display object as an icon:

   • Select . . . . ☐ Displa<u>y</u> as Icon

5 Click . . . . [OK]

   The object or object icon appears in the worksheet.

6 Click . . . . ***in worksheet***
   to deselect object and return to normal editing.
   *(Also see **Edit OLE Objects**, page 228.)*

Edit OLE Objects

NOTE: If the object was created on another computer, you can edit it only if the same source application exists locally.

1 Double-click . . . . ***object***
 *Tools and menus for the source application appear in place
 of Excel's menus and tools.*
 OR
 The source application opens displaying the object.

2 Edit . . . . ***object as desired***
 If editing object from source application,

 • Exit source application, and save if prompted.

3 Click . . . . ***in worksheet***
 to deselect object and return to normal editing.

Delete an OLE Object

1 Select . . . . ***object to delete***
2 Press . . . . **Del**

Manage Linked Objects

1 Open or select ..... *workbook containing linked object(s)*

2 Click .... **Edit, Links...**
Excel lists all source files.

To update objects set to manual:

a Select source file in .... **Source File** *list*

b Click .... | Update Now |

To open source file:

a Select source file in .... **Source File** *list*

b Click .... | Open Source |

To replace the source file with another:

a Select source file to replace in .... **Source File** *list*

b Click .... | Change Source |

c Select new source file in Change Links dialog box.

d Click .... | OK |

To change how linked objects are updated:

a Select source file in .... **Source File** *list*

b Select .... ◯ **Automatic**

OR

Select .... ◯ **Manual**

To exit dialog and return to workbook:

• Click .... | Close |

3 Click .... | OK |

Mail a Workbook

Sends a copy of the open workbook to one or more recipients.

NOTE: Requires Microsoft Exchange, Lotus cc:Mail or other mail programs compliant with Messaging Application Programming Interface (MAPI) or Vendor Independent Messaging (VIM).

1 Click . . . . **File, Send...**

2 If prompted, sign in to your mail system.

If Routing Slip prompt appears,

   a Select . . . . ◯ **Route document to . . .**

     OR

     Select . . . . ◯ **Send copy of document without using the Routing Slip**

   b Click . . . . | OK |

3 Send . . . . *message* through your mail system to one or more recipients.

Route a Workbook

Sends a copy of the open workbook all at once or sequentially to more than one recipient, then routes the workbook back to you.

NOTE: Requires Microsoft Exchange, Lotus cc:Mail or other mail programs compliant with Messaging Application Programming Interface (MAPI) or Vendor Independent Messaging (VIM).

1 Create or edit (page 231) . . . . *routing slip for workbook*

2 Click . . . . **File, Send...**

3 If prompted, sign in to your mail system.

4 Select . . . . ◯ **Route document to . . .**

5 Click . . . . | OK |

Create or Edit a Routing Slip

Creates a routing slip that is stored with the workbook. Your mail system will use the instructions in the routing slip when you route the workbook (page 230). You can also route the workbook from the Routing Slip dialog box.

1 Click .... **File, Add/Edit Routing Slip...**

2 If prompted, sign in to your mail system.

To clear routing slip:

- Select .... | Clear |

To add recipients:

a Click .... | Address... |

b Use your mail system to select recipients.
Excel adds recipients to the To list.

To remove a name from the To list:

a Select name of recipient to remove in .... **To:** *list*

b Click .... | Remove |

To re-order recipients:

a Select name of recipient to move in .... **To:** *list*

b Click .... | ▲ | or | ▼ |

c Repeat steps **a** and **b** until list is in desired order.

To change subject text:

- Type subject text in .... **Subject:** | |

To add or edit message text:

- Type message in .... **Message Text:** | |

To route workbook back to you:

- Select .... ☐ **Return When Done**

To receive notification when routing:

- Select .... ☐ **Track Status**

Continued ...

Create or Edit a Routing Slip (continued)

3 Select . . . . ○ **One After Another**

OR

Select . . . . ○ **All at Once**

4 Click . . . . | Add Slip |
to add slip to the workbook without sending.

OR

Click . . . . | Route |
to send workbook.

To reset routing slip:

NOTE: After the routed workbook is returned or the last recipient receives it, Excel changes the Clear command button to the Reset button.

- Click . . . . | Reset |

Receive Routed Workbook

NOTE: *Requires Microsoft Exchange, Lotus cc:Mail or other mail programs compliant with Messaging Application Programming Interface (MAPI) or Vendor Independent Messaging (VIM).*

– FROM YOUR MAIL PROGRAM –

1 Open .... *message containing routed workbook file*
   NOTE: *The message will indicate that the document has a routing slip and whether or not you should send the message to someone else.*

2 Open .... *attached workbook file*
   – FROM EXCEL –

3 Read or change .... *workbook data*

To send workbook to next recipient:

a Click .... **File, Send...**

b Select .... ○ **Route document to . . .**

c Click .... | OK |

To edit subject, or message text, or add recipients before sending workbook to next recipient:

a Click .... **File, Edit Routing Slip...**

b Make desired changes.

c Click .... | Route |

Record a Macro

1 If necessary, mark (page 235) .. *position for recording macro*

2 Click .... **Tools, Record Macro ▶**

then click .... **Record New Macro...**

3 Type macro name in .... **Macro Name:** ☐

4 Type description in .... **Description:** ☐

5 Click .... ☐ Options >>

To assign macro to Tools menu:

a Select .... ☐ **Menu Item on Tools Menu**

b Type menu text in .. **Menu Item on Tools Menu:** ☐

To assign a shortcut key for playing back macro:

a Select .... ☐ **Shortcut Key**

b Type letter in .... **Ctrl +** ☐

To specify where macro will be stored:

• Select .... *Store in option:*
Personal Macro Workbook — macro will always be available.
This Workbook — macro will only be available in current workbook.
New Workbook — stores macro in separate workbook.

To set macro language:

• Select .. ◯ **Visual Basic** or ◯ **MS Excel 4.0 Macro**

6 Click .... ☐ OK
Excel displays a tool bar with a Stop Macro button.

To set references to relative or absolute:

a Click .... **Tools, Record Macro ▶**

b Select or deselect .... **Use Relative References**

7 Execute .... *commands to record*

8 Click .... *Stop Macro button* ☐
when done.
*Excel adds a module or macro sheet to the end of the existing sheets
in the workbook if you specified This Workbook, above.*

Play Back a Macro

- Press . . . . *assigned shortcut key*

OR

1 Click . . . . **Tools, Macro...**

2 Select macro to run in . . . . **Macro Name/Reference:** *list*

3 Click . . . . [Run]

OR

1 Click . . . . **Tools**

2 Select . . . . *assigned macro name* near bottom of menu.

Mark Position for Recording Macro

Marks starting point in a module where a new macro will be recorded or marks insertion point where recorded actions will be inserted into an existing macro.

1 Select . . . . *module sheet containing macro*

2 Place . . . . *insertion point in module* where macro code will be inserted or new macro will begin.

3 Click . . . . **Tools, Record Macro ▶** then click . . . . **Mark Position for Recording**

4 Select . . . . *sheet and cell where recording will begin*

5 Record macro (page 234) or record actions into existing macro (see below).

Record Actions into Existing Macro

1 Mark (see above) . . . . *position in existing macro* where macro code will be inserted.
   NOTE: *If using MS Excel 4.0 macro language, insert cells in module to receive macro code. (You will need to edit the macro when done.)*

2 Click . . . . **Tools, Record Macro ▶, Record at Mark**

3 Follow steps to Record a Macro (below step 6), page 234.

Assign Macro to a Graphic Button

1 Click . . . . *Drawing button* 🔲
on Standard toolbar to show Drawing toolbar.

2 Click . . . . *Create Button* ▢
on Drawing toolbar.
Pointer becomes a ╋

3 Drag . . . . *outline of button*
to desired position in worksheet.

4 Select desired macro in . . . . . . **Macro Name/Reference:** *list*

5 Click . . . . | OK |

6 Click in . . . . *button text*

7 Edit . . . . *text in button*

8 Click . . . . *in worksheet*
NOTE: *To select a button to which a macro has been assigned,
you must first click the Drawing Selection button* ▨ *on the Drawing
toolbar. This will let you select the button without executing the macro.*

Manage Existing Macros

1 Click . . . . **Tools, Macro...**

2 Select macro name in . . . . **Macro Name/Reference:** *list*

To edit macro code:

● Click . . . . | Edit |

To delete selected Visual Basic macro:

● Click . . . . | Delete |

To set options for selected macro:

a Click . . . . | Options... |

b Select . . . . **Macro options:**
*Description, Assign to Menu Item on Tools Menu,
Assign to Shortcut Key, Function Category, Status Bar Text,
Help Context ID, Help File Name*

c Click . . . . | OK |

3 Click . . . . | Close |

Create Text Notes

1 Select . . . . *cell to attach note to*

2 Click . . . . **Insert, No̲te...**

3 Type note in . . . . **T̲ext Note:** *box*

To add notes to other cells:

a Click . . . . | A̲dd |

b Select (in worksheet) or
type cell reference for note in . . . . **C̲ell:** | |

c Type note in . . . . **T̲ext Note:** *box*
NOTE: You can edit or delete existing text in T̲ext Note box.

d Repeat steps **a-c**, as needed.

4 Click . . . . | OK |
Excel marks each cell containing a note with a note marker (small square).

Show or Play Back Note

- Point to . . . . *cell containing note*
NOTE: Cells with notes have a small square in upper-right corner.
Excel displays text and/or plays back sound in note.

Edit Text Notes

1 Click . . . . **Insert, No̲te...**

2 Select cell containing note in . . . . **Notes in S̲heet:** *list*

3 View or edit note in . . . . **T̲ext Note:** *box*

4 Repeat steps **2** and **3**, as needed.

5 Click . . . . | OK |

Create Sound Notes

NOTE: Requires installation of a sound card and driver.

Using a Sound File

1 Select . . . . ***cell to attach note to***

2 Click . . . . **Insert, No̲te...**

3 Click . . . . | I̲mport... |

4 Select sound file in . . . . ***Import Sound dialog box***

5 Click . . . . | OK |

*NOTE: To attach a different sound file to the note,
click Erase then repeat steps 3-5.*

To add the same sound note to other cells:

a Click . . . . | A̲dd |

b Select (in worksheet) or
type cell reference for note in . . . . **C̲ell:** | |

c Repeat steps **a** and **b**, as needed.
*Excel marks references containing attached sound notes
with an asterisk (*) in Notes in S̲heet list.*

6 Click . . . . | OK |

Excel marks cells containing notes with note markers (small squares).

By Recording a Sound

1 Select . . . . ***cell to attach note to***

2 Click . . . . **Insert, No̲te...**

3 Click . . . . | Record... |

*NOTE: The Record button is not available if cell
already has a sound note attached to it.*

4 Click . . . . | ● |
Record

5 Record . . . . ***note***

NOTE: To pause the recording, click the Pause button.

Continued ...

Create Sound Notes — By Recording a Sound (continued)

6 Click . . . . ▪️
    Stop

    NOTE: *To test the recording, click the Play button.*

7 Click . . . . [OK]

    NOTE: *To attach a different recording to the note,*
    click Erase then repeat steps 3-7.

To add the same sound note to other cells:

a Click . . . . [A̲dd]

b Select (in worksheet) or
    type cell reference for note in . . . . **C̲ell:** [   ]

c Repeat steps **a** and **b**, as needed.
    Excel marks references containing attached sound notes
    with an asterisk (*) in Notes in S̲heet list.

8 Click . . . . [OK]

Play Back Sounds Attached to Notes

1 Click . . . . **I̲nsert, No̲te...**

2 Select cell containing an asterisk (*) in . . . . **Notes in S̲heet:** *list*

3 Click . . . . [P̲lay]

4 Repeat steps **2** and **3**, as needed.

5 Click . . . . [OK]

Erase Sounds Attached to Notes

Retains the text in a note that has both text and sound.

1 Click .... **Insert, Note...**

2 Select note containing an asterisk (*) in ... **Notes in Sheet:** *list*

3 Click .... | Erase |

Excel changes the Erase button to Record after sound has been erased.

NOTE: The asterisk (*) will remain until you exit the dialog box.

To erase sounds in other cells:

a Click .... | Add |

b Select note containing an asterisk (*) in . **Notes in Sheet:** *list*

c Click .... | Erase |

d Repeat steps **a-c**, as needed.

4 Click .... | OK |

Delete Notes

1 Select .... *cell(s) containing note(s)*

2 Click .... **Edit, Clear ▸, Notes**

OR

1 Click .... **Insert, Note...**

2 Select note to delete in .... **Notes in Sheet:** *list*

3 Click .... | Delete |

4 Click .... | OK |

to confirm deletion.

5 Repeat steps **2-4**, as needed.

6 Click .... | Close |

Use Info Window to View or Print Cell Details

1 Click . . . . **T̲ools, O̲ptions...**

FROM VIEW

2 Select . . . . ☐ **Info W̲indow**

3 Click . . . . [OK]

4 Click . . . . **W̲indow, A̲rrange...**

5 Select . . . . *Arrange option:*
T̲iled, Ho̲rizontal, V̲ertical

6 Click . . . . [OK]

To add or remove information displayed:

a Select . . . . *Info window*

b Click . . . . **I̲nfo**
on menu bar.
NOTE: *Check marks appear next to selected categories.*

c Select or deselect . . . . *information category:*
C̲ell, Fo̲rmula, V̲alue, Forma̲t, Pro̲tection,
Na̲mes, P̲recedents..., De̲pendents..., N̲ote

If Precedents or Dependents,

1. Select . . . . ◯ **D̲irect Only** or ◯ **A̲ll Levels**

2. Click . . . . [OK]

d Repeat steps **b** and **c** for each category to add or remove.

7 Select . . . . *cell in any worksheet*
to view its details in Info window.

To print Info window information:

a Select . . . . *cells in worksheet*
containing information to print.

b Select . . . . *Info window*

c Click . . . . *Print button* 🖨

Close Info Window

- Click . . . . *Info window's close button*

Audit Worksheet

Excel's audit commands use arrows to trace precedents (cells referred to by formulas) and dependents (cells containing formulas that refer to the active cell). You can use these tools to debug your worksheet formulas. Tracer arrows are not saved with the workbook.

Show Auditing Toolbar

- Click . . . **Tools, Auditing ▸, Show Auditing Toolbar**

Trace Dependent Formulas

1 Select . . . . . *cell containing data referred to by a formula*

2 Click . . . . *Trace Dependents button*
on Auditing toolbar (*see above*).
*NOTE: If Tracer arrows do not appear, see **Set View Options**, page 179, and deselect the Hi*d*e All option.*

Remove Dependent Tracer Arrows

1 Select . . . . *cell containing data used by a formula*

2 Click . . . . *Remove Dependent Arrows button*
on Auditing toolbar (*see above*).

Trace Precedent Data and Formulas

1 Select . . . . *cell containing formula*

2 Click . . . . *Trace Precedents button*
on Auditing toolbar (*see above*).
*NOTE: If Tracer arrows do not appear, see **Set View Options**, page 179, and deselect the Hi*d*e All option.*

Remove Precedent Tracer Arrows

1 Select . . . . *cell containing formula*

2 Click . . . . *Remove Precedent Arrows button*
on Auditing toolbar *(page 242).*

Remove All Tracer Arrows

• Click . . . . *Remove All Arrows button*
on Auditing toolbar *(page 242).*

Select Cell at End of Tracer Arrows

1 Double-click . . . . *tracer arrow*

2 Repeat step **1** to select cell at opposite end.

Trace Possible Error
Source in a Formula

1 Click . . . . *cell containing error value*

2 Click . . . . *Trace Error button*
on Auditing toolbar *(page 242).*

About Cells

Cells are areas in a worksheet in which data is stored. Each cell is defined by the intersection of a row and column (such as A3, denoting column A, row 3). A **cell reference** identifies a cell or a range of cells.

About Formulas

Formulas are mathematical expressions that create new values by combining numerical values with operators (plus, minus, etc.). Formulas may contain cell references (relative, absolute, or mixed), operators, and functions. See the topics that follow.

Relative Cell References

A relative cell reference (such as A2) describes a cell's location based on its relationship to another cell.

Formula example: =**A2***10

This formula multiplies the contents of cell A2 by 10. The cell reference A2 will change to B2 if you copy this formula one cell position to the right. The copied formula will become =**B2***10.

Absolute Cell References

An absolute cell reference (such as $A$2) describes an exact cell location. Use a dollar sign ($) before both the column letter and the row number to specify an absolute cell reference.

Formula example: =**$A$2**10

This formula multiplies the contents of cell A2 by 10. The cell reference $A$2 will not change if you copy the formula to another cell. The copied formula would remain =**$A$2***10.

Mixed Cell References

A **mixed cell reference** (such as $A2) describes a cell location with relative and absolute parts. The dollar sign ($) marks the absolute part of the reference while the unmarked part (2) defines the relative part of the reference.

Formula example: =$A2*10

This formula multiplies the contents of cell A2 by 10. Only the relative part of the cell reference will adjust if you copy the formula one cell position to the right. The copied formula would become =$A3*10.

Cell References (Examples)

The tables that follow contain examples of reference operators in cell references. You can also use named references with these operators.

References to cells in the <u>same worksheet</u>

Colons (:) between references indicate a range of cells between and including the two references.

Commas (,) between references indicate a union (one reference that includes the two references) of the cells.

A space between references indicate a single cell location where the two references intersect.

To refer to:	Reference examples
a **range** of cells (adjacent cells)	C5:E5
a **union** of non-adjacent cells	C5,E5
an **intersection** of two ranges	C5:C10 A7:E7
all of **column C**	C:C
all of **row 3**	3:3
all of **rows 3 through 5**	3:5
the **entire worksheet**	A:IV *or* 1:16384
a named reference, "sales"	sales

References to cells in <u>another worksheet</u>

Exclamation signs (!) separate the sheet name from the cell reference.

Colons (:) between worksheet names indicate a range of worksheets. Use **quotation marks** if worksheet name contains a space.

To refer to:	Reference examples
cells in a **different worksheet** (Sales 93)	"Sales 93"!A1:D1
a **3-D reference** to cells in range of worksheets (A1 on sheets Sheet1 through Sheet3)	Sheet1:Sheet3!A1

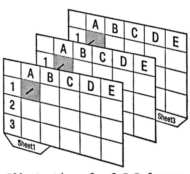

Illustration of a 3-D Reference

References to cells in <u>another workbook</u> (External References or Links)

Single quotations (') enclose the path, filename, and sheet-level name when creating a sheet-level reference.

Square brackets ([ ]) enclose the workbook filename.

Exclamation signs (!) separate the sheet name from the cell reference.

To refer to:	Reference examples
cells in a **different workbook** (sheet-level)	'c:\excel\[sales.xls]sheet2'!D1:D10
named cells in a **different workbook** (book-level).	'c:\excel\[sales.xls]'!sales

Arithmetic Operators

Arithmetic operators direct Excel to carry out mathematical operations. The following is a list of arithmetic operators that can be used in formulas:

+	Addition	*****	Multiplication
-	Subtraction	**/**	Division
%	Percentage of	**^**	Exponentiation

Formula example: `=2*(A1+B4)`

This formula calculates and displays the sum of values contained in cells `A1` and `B4`, multiplied by `2`.

Comparison Operators

Comparison operators compare values and produce the logical value TRUE or FALSE. The following is a list of comparison operators that can be used in formulas:

=	Equal
>=	Greater than or equal to
>	Greater than
<=	Less than or equal to
<	Less than
<>	Not equal to

Formula example: `=IF(A1=B2,"equal","unequal")`

This formula compares values contained in cells `A1` and `B2`, then displays `equal` if it is true (that `A1` equals `B2`); if not, it displays `unequal`.

Text Operator

A text operator combines text values into one value. Use an ampersand (&) to combine text values.

Formula example: =A1&B10

This formula combines and displays text contained in cells A1 and B10. If cell A1 contains MICRO, and B10 contains SOFT, the result of this formula would be MICROSOFT.

About Worksheet Functions

Worksheet functions are prewritten formulas that can be used alone or as part of a formula. Use the Paste function command from the Formula menu to list the many functions Excel provides.

The following are some examples of worksheet functions to be used with Excel:

> AVERAGE(number1,number2,...)
>
> NPV(rate,value1,value2,...)
>
> SUM(number1,number2,...)

Formula example: =AVERAGE(A1:B10)

This formula calculates and displays the mean average of values contained in the cell range A1:B10.

NOTE: *The* **Function Wizard** *helps you to build and understand functions. It lets you select functions from the following categories:*

Most Recently Used	*All*
Financial	*Date & Time*
Math and Trig	*Statistical*
Lookup & Reference	*Database*
Text	*Logical*
Information	

Using Functions to Evaluate Conditions

The IF function and the AND, OR, and NOT logical functions are useful for evaluating cell contents and can be used together to evaluate complex conditions:

IF(condition,true,false)   OR(condition)

NOT(condition)   AND(condition)

In the examples that follow, the cell containing the value 90 has been named **Temp** and the cell containing the value 70 has been named **Hum**. In the first sample function below, the IF function returns the first value ("HOT") because the condition (Temp >=90) is <u>true</u>.

Temp	Hum
90	70

Sample function:	*Returns:*
`=IF(`<u>`Temp>=90`</u>`,"`<u>`HOT`</u>`","NOT HOT")`	*HOT*
`=NOT(Temp=67)`	*TRUE*
`=IF(AND(Temp>=90,Hum>=70),"SULTRY","OK")`	*SULTRY*
`=IF(OR(Temp>=90,Hum>=80),"STICKY","OK")`	*STICKY*
`=IF(NOT(Temp=90),"IT IS NOT 90","IT'S 90")`	*IT'S 90*

Checking for Numbers in Cells

The ISNUMBER function is useful for checking to see if a cell contains a number. In the example that follows, the ISNUMBER function is used with the IF function to check if cell B3 contains a number. If B3 contains a number (evaluates to **true**), the IF function multiplies B3 by 10 (B3*10). If B3 is not a number, the IF function returns the character value "Not a Number."

Sample function:

`=IF(ISNUMBER(B3),`**`B3*10`**`,"Not a Number")`

   If the contents of B3 is 10, returns 100

   If the contents of B3 is not a number, returns "Not a Number"

Using the AND Function
to Evaluate Two Conditions

The AND function is useful for checking two conditions. For example, you can use the AND function with the IF function to perform a calculation only if *both* cells contains a number. In the example that follows, the ISNUMBER function checks to see if cell B2 *and* cell B3 contain a number. If both contain numbers (evaluate to *true*), the IF function multiplies B2 by B3. If either cell does not contain a number, the IF function returns the character value "Not Numbers."

NOTE: *When combining (nesting) functions like this, be careful to include the required parentheses. It's easy to leave one out!*

Sample function:

```
=IF(AND(ISNUMBER(B2),ISNUMBER(B3)),B2*B3,"Not Numbers")
```

If B2 is 10 and B3 is 20, returns 200
If B2 and B3 are not numbers, returns "Not Numbers"

NOTE: *You can use the OR function instead of the AND function if either (not both) conditions must be true before the IF function carries out the specified action.*

How Excel Adjusts References

When you create formulas that reference cells, and then make changes to the worksheet (like moving cells or inserting rows or columns), Excel will often adjust the references relative to the number of cells involved in the action.

Action:	Reference adjustment:
Move cells	Absolute and relative references adjust.
Copy cells	Relative references adjust. Absolute references are retained.
Insert/delete cells	All reference types adjust.
Insert/delete sheets within a 3-D reference*	3-D reference adjusts. For example, if you delete a sheet within a 3-D reference, the reference will include only the remaining sheets.
Move sheets at either end of a 3-D reference*	3-D reference adjusts. For example, if you move a sheet that ends a reference, six positions to the right, the 3-D reference will include all sheets between the two sheets.

** 3-D references are indicated by a starting and ending sheet name. Here is an example of a 3-D reference in a formula: =SUM(**Sheet1:Sheet4**!A1:D5). The 3-D reference includes the range of cells A1:D5 in the worksheets* **Sheet1** *through* **Sheet4***.*

ERROR MESSAGES: *If an error message occurs after you change a worksheet, refer to* **Formula Error Messages and Possible Causes**, *on the following page.*

Formula Error Messages and Possible Causes

Below is a list of error values that may appear in cells when Excel cannot calculate the formula for that cell.

#DIV/0!   Indicates that the formula is trying to divide by zero.

In formula: • Divisor is a zero. • Divisor is referring to a blank cell or a cell that contains a zero value.

#N/A   Indicates that no value is available.

In formula: • An invalid argument may have been used with a LOOKUP function. • A reference in an array formula does not match range in which results are displayed. • A required argument has been omitted from a function.

#NAME?   Indicates that Excel does not recognize the name used in a formula.

In formula: • A named reference has been deleted or has not been defined. • A function or name reference has been misspelled. • Text has been entered without required quotation marks. • A colon has been omitted in a range reference.

#NULL!   Indicates that the intersection of two range references does not exist.

In formula: • Two range references (separated with a space operator) have been used to represent a non-existent intersection of the two ranges.

#NUM!   Indicates a number error.

In formula: • An incorrect value has been used in a function. • Arguments result in a number too small or large to be represented.

Continued

Formula Error Messages and Possible Causes (continued)

#REF!   Indicates reference to an invalid cell.

In formula: • Arguments refer to cells that have been deleted or overwritten with non-numeric data. The argument is replaced with #REF!.

#VALUE!   Indicates the invalid use of an operator or argument.

In formula: • An invalid value or a referenced value has been used with a formula or function (i.e., SUM("John")).

Circular   A message that indicates formula is referencing itself.

In formula: • A cell reference refers to the cell containing the formula result.

NOTE: *If a circular reference is intended, you can select the **Iteration** option (page 96). Iteration is an instruction to repeat a calculation until a specific result value is met.*

In most cases, the noun is the primary index key.
For example, look up "Sheets, select" instead of "Select, sheets."

In most cases, the noun is the primary index key.
For example, look up "Sheets, select" instead of "Select, sheets."

In most cases, the noun is the primary index key.
For example, look up "Sheets, select" instead of "Select, sheets."

In most cases, the noun is the primary index key.
For example, look up "Sheets, select" instead of "Select, sheets."

In most cases, the noun is the primary index key.
For example, look up "Sheets, select" instead of "Select, sheets."

In most cases, the noun is the primary index key.
For example, look up "Sheets, select" instead of "Select, sheets."

F

In most cases, the noun is the primary index key.
For example, look up "Sheets, select" instead of "Select, sheets."

In most cases, the noun is the primary index key.
For example, look up "Sheets, select" instead of "Select, sheets."

In most cases, the noun is the primary index key.
For example, look up "Sheets, select" instead of "Select, sheets."

In most cases, the noun is the primary index key.
For example, look up "Sheets, select" instead of "Select, sheets."

In most cases, the noun is the primary index key.
For example, look up "Sheets, select" instead of "Select, sheets."

Q R

In most cases, the noun is the primary index key.
For example, look up "Sheets, select" instead of "Select, sheets."

In most cases, the noun is the primary index key.
For example, look up "Sheets, select" instead of "Select, sheets."

In most cases, the noun is the primary index key.
For example, look up "Sheets, select" instead of "Select, sheets."

*In most cases, the noun is the primary index key.
For example, look up "Sheets, select" instead of "Select, sheets."*

Z

In most cases, the noun is the primary index key.
For example, look up "Sheets, select" instead of "Select, sheets."

FREE CATALOG
&
UPDATED LISTING

We don't just have books that find your answers faster; we also have books that teach you how to use your computer without the fairy tales and the gobbledygook.

We also have books to improve your typing, spelling and punctuation.

Tear out the slip below and return it to us for a free catalog and mailing list update.

RETURN TODAY!

- -

DDC *Publishing*

14 E. 38th St. New York, NY 10016

❑ Please send me your catalog and put me on your mailing list.

_____
Name

_____
Firm (if any)

_____
Address

_____
City, State, Zip

More Quick Reference Guide

Access 2 for Win.................................0-AX2	Quattro Pro 4 for DOS........................
Ami Pro 3 for Win................................Z-18	Quattro Pro 5 for Win..................0-QI
DOS 5...J-17	Quicken 3 for Win.......................0-QI
DOS 6.0 - 6.22..............................0-DS62	Quicken 4 for Win..........................
Excel 4 for Win..................................A-18	Quicken 7 for DOS.........................0-
Excel 5 for Win...................................F-18	Windows 3.1 & 3.11........................N
Internet..I-17	Windows for Workgroups..............W
Laptops & Notebooks LM-18	Word 6.0 for Win......................0-W
Lotus 1-2-3 Rel. 3.1 DOS..................J-18	WordPerfect 5.1+ for DOS...............V
Lotus 1-2-3 Rel. 3.4 DOS L3-17	WordPerfect 5.1/5.2 for Win............
Lotus 1-2-3 Rel. 4.0 DOS...................G-4	WordPerfect 6.0 for DOS.................\
Lotus 1-2-3 Rel. 4.0 Win................0-301-3	WordPerfect 6.0 for Win.............0-W
Lotus 1-2-3 Rel. 5.0 Win L-19	WordPerfect 6.1 for Win................\
Lotus Notes 3..................................0-LN3	
Microsoft Office................................MO-17	
MS Works 2 for Win...........................H-18	**Desktop Publishing**
MS Works 3 for DOS M-18	Word 2.0 for Win ....
MS Works 3 for Win.......................0-WKW3	Word 6.0 for Win.............................
Office Reference Manual......................R-88	WordPerfect 5.1 for DOS ....
PageMaker 5 for Win & Mac PM-18	WordPerfect 6.0 for Win ....
Paradox 4.5 for Win PW-18	Graphic Design/
PowerPoint 4.0 for Win 0-PPW4	Desktop Publishing......................

---------- ORDER FORM ----------

DDC Publishing   14 E. 38 St., NY, NY 10016   **$10**e

QTY.	CAT. NO.	DESCRIPTION

☐ Check enclosed. Add $2.50 for post. & handling & $1 post. for ea. add. gu
NY State res. add local sales tax.

☐ Visa   ☐ Mastercard   *100% Refund Guaran*

No._____Exp._____

Name_____

Firm _____

Address_____

City, State, Zip _____

Phone (800)528-3897   Fax (800)528-3862